The Vegetarian Pasta Cookbook

TARRAGON

The
Vegetarian
Pasta
Cookbook

*A superb selection of delicious
and nutritious pasta dishes*

SARAH MAXWELL

APPLE

A QUINTET BOOK

Published by The Apple Press
6 Blundell Street London, N7 9BH

ISBN 1–85076–507–3

Reprinted 1997, 1998
This book was designed and produced by
Quintet Publishing Limited
6 Blundell Street
London N7 9BH

Creative Director: Richard Dewing
Designer: Ian Hunt
Project Editor: Katie Preston
Editor: Diana Vowles
Illustrator: Shona Cameron
Photographer: Tim Hill
Home Economist: Sarah Maxwell
Assistant Home Economist: Teresa Goldfinch

Typeset in Great Britain by
Central Southern Typesetters, Eastbourne
Manufactured in Singapore by Eray Scan Pte Ltd
Printed in Hong Kong by
Sing Cheong Printing Co. Ltd.

DEDICATION
For Paul and Oliver
And with special thanks to my mum, Jenny

Contents

Introduction

TORTELLINI

BELOW *Three flavours of fresh pasta noodles ready for storing.*

The Vegetarian Pasta Cookbook provides you with exciting, new and interesting recipes, some of which are quick and simple to prepare while others require a little extra time and effort for those special-occasion meals. Whether you're cooking for a group of vegetarian guests or the odd one out in the family, these recipes will give you plenty of mouthwatering ideas.

The chapters have been divided into categories of ingredients for quick and easy reference – so when you fancy making pasta with tomatoes, for example, simply turn to Pasta with Tomatoes and there are plenty of variations to choose from. There are recipes for all occasions, from fast family suppers to formal food for friends. So take the plunge and boil up some pasta to be turned into a delicious vegetarian feast.

A word about the final chapter, Pasta Puddings. Don't be shy – have a go and you (and your guests) are guaranteed to be pleasantly surprised.

The vegetarian issue

Although this book is predominantly suited to the lacto-vegetarian, there are a few vegan recipes also included.

Vegetarian cheeses made with vegetable rennet are becoming increasingly available in many different flavours and textures. If the particular cheeses recommended in the recipes are not available in a vegetarian form, you can simply use another type.

A point to note is to beware of certain coloured pastas which are not vegetarian. For example, black pasta will probably be dyed with squid ink.

PASTA

Pasta is one of man's earliest culinary inventions, dating back to over 3,000 years ago when the ancient Greeks recorded it in manuscripts and paintings, showing it to be one of the staple foods in their diet. Greece and Italy are not the only countries with a history of pasta making – the tradition also exists in Spain, Israel and even Russia.

Pasta (which means paste in Italian) is generally made from semolina, durum or hard wheat mixed with water and/or oil and sometimes eggs. The dough is kneaded and rolled or extruded commercially to produce a myriad of shapes and sizes.

Fresh pasta is becoming even more available in many different varieties, not only from delicatessens (where the pasta is often made on the premises) but also from major supermarkets, where it can be found in packets in the chilled cabinets.

The type of complex carbohydrates found in pasta makes it a good energy food, providing the body with a steady flow of energy as the carbohydrates are broken down during digestion.

Mix and match

It is a case of personal preference when it comes to choosing a particular pasta shape to match your favourite pasta sauce. You may prefer small gnocchi (shells) to scoop up a rich tomato sauce and tagliatelle or linguini for serving with a thick, creamy sauce, where each strand of pasta can be evenly coated in the sauce for a perfect combination of flavour and texture.

There continues to be great confusion over certain names for certain shapes of pasta. Suffice it to say that if you are able to describe its shape rather than remember its name, you are more likely to get what you are after!

Nutrition

Contrary to popular belief, pasta is not a fattening food. It is actually said to be quite low in calories and high in fibre, B vitamins and minerals such as potassium and iron.

ROTELLE

R I G H T *Freshly prepared farfalle (pasta bows).*

Pasta Dough

This is the basic recipe referred to throughout the book. The dough can be made up to 2 days in advance, if kept airtight in the fridge. Bring the dough to room temperature before rolling out.

Freezing pasta is best done after it has been rolled out and cut into the required shape. Cook from frozen, allowing a little extra cooking time for stuffed pasta shapes.

MAKES ABOUT 550G/1¼LB

350g/12oz strong plain flour

1tbsp salt

60ml/4tbsp sunflower oil

12ml/1tbsp water

3 eggs

In a large mixing bowl, combine the flour and salt. Make a well in the centre. In a mixing jug, combine the sunflower oil and water and beat well. Break the eggs into the well and add the oil and water mixture gradually. Mix until the dough forms clumps.

Turn out on to a lightly floured surface and knead the dough for about 5 minutes, adding the minimum amount of extra flour to stop the dough sticking, if necessary.

Place the dough in a polythene bag or seal in clingfilm and leave to rest, at room temperature, for at least 30 minutes.

Roll out the dough and cut to any shape you require.

TIPS FOR COOKING PERFECT PASTA:

- Use good-quality pasta.

- Use a saucepan which is large enough to hold the pasta with the water and still have at least one third of the saucepan free.

- Bring the water to the boil before adding the pasta, then simmer for the duration of the cooking time.

- Add a dash of oil to the cooking water to help prevent the pasta sticking together.

- Cook the pasta until *al dente,* or tender.

- To halt the cooking process, drain the pasta through a sieve and rinse under cold running water.

BASIC SAUCES

These basic sauces are used in recipes throughout the book. However, they can also be used as recipes in their own right, poured over or mixed into your favourite pasta shapes. Made up to two days in advance and kept, covered in the refrigerator, the sauces can be reheated for use in the recipes.

Cheese Sauce

This sauce will keep in the fridge covered, for up to a week. Use for lasagnes, bakes, toppings and fillings.

MAKES ABOUT 575ML/1PT

25g/1oz butter or margarine

25g/1oz plain flour

575ml/1pt warm milk

5ml/1tsp Dijon mustard

100g/4oz grated mature Cheddar cheese

salt and freshly ground black pepper

Melt the butter or margarine in a medium-sized saucepan and stir in the flour. Cook for 30 seconds then remove from the heat.

Stir in the milk, a little at a time, blending well after each addition to prevent any lumps. Return the sauce to a medium heat and stir constantly until the sauce thickens and boils.

Add the mustard and cheese and season to taste with salt and freshly ground black pepper. Continue to cook, stirring constantly, until the cheese has melted.

VARIATIONS:

MUSHROOM SAUCE Omit the mustard and cheese and stir in 175g/6oz chopped button mushrooms which have been sautéed in a little olive oil with a clove of crushed garlic and a pinch of dried thyme.

TOMATO SAUCE Omit the mustard and cheese and stir in 45ml/3tbsp tomato purée.

RAVIOLI

Pesto Sauce

This traditional Italian sauce should be used in moderation as it has a very strong flavour. Delicious stirred into fresh pasta, Pesto Sauce can also be used as an ingredient, added to other sauces and dishes. The texture of the finished pesto can be left quite coarse or puréed until smooth.

SERVES 4–6

2 cloves of garlic, crushed

8tbsp chopped fresh basil

2tbsp chopped fresh parsley

50g/2oz pine nuts

75g/3oz fresh grated Parmesan cheese

150ml/¼pt extra virgin olive oil

salt and freshly ground black pepper

Place all the ingredients in a food processor or blender and blend until the pesto reaches the desired texture.

Stir Pesto Sauce into freshly cooked pasta tossed in butter and freshly ground black pepper. Serve immediately with extra freshly grated Parmesan cheese.

TIP:
For a more traditional method of preparation, place all the ingredients in a mortar and use the pestle to grind and pound until the pesto reaches the desired texture.

BASIL

Cream Sauce

An excellent standby sauce for any occasion. It is delicious served with spaghetti or used as a foundation for other ingredients to make a more elaborate dish.

SERVES 4

2 cloves of garlic, crushed

3tbsp chopped fresh parsley

275ml/½pt single cream

salt and freshly ground black pepper

Place all the ingredients in a medium-sized frying pan and cook over low heat for 5–8 minutes, stirring occasionally.

SERVING SUGGESTION:
Stir Cream Sauce into freshly cooked tagliatelle verde and serve immediately with plenty of freshly grated Parmesan cheese.

PARSLEY

Pasta *with Mushrooms*

Nutty Mushroom Bake

Most types of pasta work well for the topping of this dish; try spaghetti or tagliatelle instead of pennoni.

FIELD

SERVES 4

175g/6oz dried pennoni (quills)

dash of olive oil, plus 30ml/2tbsp

25g/1oz butter

1 onion, chopped

1 clove of garlic, crushed

2tsp dried oregano

275g/10oz cup mushrooms, sliced

400g/14oz can chopped tomatoes

25g/1oz tomato purée

50g/2oz pimiento-stuffed green olives, sliced

75g/3oz roasted cashew nuts

salt and freshly ground black pepper

100g/4oz grated mature Cheddar cheese

Bring a large saucepan of water to the boil and add the pennoni with a dash of olive oil. Cook for about 10 minutes, stirring occasionally, until tender. Drain, return to the saucepan and stir in the butter until melted. Set aside, covered.

Preheat the oven to 200°C/400°F/Gas Mark 6. Heat the remaining oil in a large frying pan and sauté the onion, garlic and oregano for 3 minutes, or until the onion has softened.

Add the sliced mushrooms and cook for a further 5 minutes, stirring occasionally. Stir in the chopped tomatoes and the tomato purée. Cover and cook for about 10 minutes, stirring occasionally.

Add the sliced olives and the cashew nuts and season with salt and freshly ground black pepper. Continue to cook for a final 2–3 minutes, then transfer the mixture to a shallow, ovenproof dish. Spoon the buttered pasta on top and sprinkle with the cheese. Bake for 20 minutes, or until crisp and golden.

Herby Mushroom Pasta Salad

Any small pasta shapes would be suitable for this dish. It can be served as a filling main course at lunchtime or as an accompaniment.

SERVES 4–8

450g/1lb dried pasta shapes

dash of olive oil

225g/8oz cup mushrooms, quartered

1 red pepper, seeded and cut into 1cm/½inch squares

1 yellow pepper, seeded and cut into 1cm/½inch squares

100g/4oz pitted black olives

4tbsp chopped fresh basil

2tbsp chopped fresh parsley

FOR THE DRESSING:

10ml/2tsp red wine vinegar

1tsp salt

freshly ground black pepper

60ml/4tbsp extra virgin olive oil

1 clove of garlic, crushed

5–10ml/1–2tsp Dijon mustard

Bring a large saucepan of water to the boil and add the pasta shapes with a dash of olive oil. Cook for about 10 minutes, stirring occasionally, until tender. Drain and rinse under cold running water. Drain well again.

Place the cooked pasta shapes in a large salad bowl and add the remaining salad ingredients. Mix well to combine.

To make the dressing, place all the ingredients in a screw-top jar and shake well. Pour the dressing over the salad and toss together.

Cover and refrigerate for at least 30 minutes, then toss again before serving.

PARSLEY

Clear Cep Soup

This is a formal soup for special occasions. It has a strong mushroom flavour with the delicate addition of vegetables and pasta to create the contrasting textures.

SERVES 4

25g/1oz dried ceps

575ml/1pt warm water

1 leek

1 carrot

75g/3oz conchigliette piccole (tiny pasta shells), cooked

salt and freshly ground black pepper

flat parsley leaves to garnish

Place the ceps in the warm water and leave to soak for about 30 minutes. Drain the ceps, reserving the liquid in a saucepan.

Slice the ceps and shred the leek and carrot. Add the vegetables to the mushroom stock and cook over medium heat for about 10 minutes, until the vegetables are tender. Add the cooked pasta shells and season with salt and freshly ground black pepper. Cook for a further minute. Serve garnished with parsley leaves.

Farfalle with Fontina

Fontina cheese is available from most good cheese shops and gives this dish a creamy, subtle flavour. Although Emmental cheese is not a perfect substitute, it is more readily available and can be used as a good alternative.

SERVES 4

375g/13oz dried farfalle (bows)

dash of olive oil

75g/3oz butter

1 onion, finely chopped

3tbsp chopped fresh basil

225g/8oz cup mushrooms, sliced

400g/14oz can chopped tomatoes

200g/7oz coarsely grated Fontina cheese

salt and freshly ground black pepper

Bring a large saucepan of water to the boil and add the farfalle with a dash of olive oil. Cook for about 10 minutes, stirring occasionally, until tender. Drain and set aside, covered, to keep warm.

Melt the butter in a large frying pan and sauté the onion and basil for about 5 minutes until the onion is tender but not browned.

Stir the mushrooms into the onion mixture and continue to cook for a further 5–8 minutes, stirring frequently, until the mushrooms begin to brown.

Add the chopped tomatoes to the mushroom mixture and cook for 1–2 minutes. Stir in the cheese and season to taste with salt and freshly ground black pepper. Cook for a further 3–4 minutes, until the cheese has melted. Serve with the cooked farfalle.

FARFALLE

Clear Cep Soup

Pasta-topped Mushrooms

This dish is delicious served cold with a crisp leafy salad or warm as a starter or an accompaniment. The topping can be made in advance and arranged on the mushrooms at the last minute.

SERVES 2–4

50g/2oz dried small stellette (stars)

dash of olive oil

4 large flat mushrooms

50g/2oz butter

1 clove of garlic, crushed

½ yellow pepper, seeded and finely diced

½ orange pepper, seeded and finely diced

150g/5oz blue cheese, such as Stilton or Danish blue, crumbled

salt and freshly ground black pepper

2tbsp chopped fresh parsley

Bring a large saucepan of water to the boil and add the stellette with a dash of olive oil. Cook for about 7 minutes, stirring occasionally, until tender. Drain and set aside.

Cut the stalks out of the mushrooms and discard. Arrange the mushrooms, stalk side up, on a baking sheet and set aside.

To make the topping, melt the butter in a frying pan and sauté the garlic for about 2 minutes. Add the diced peppers and cook for a further 5–7 minutes. Stir in the crumbled blue cheese and season to taste with salt and freshly ground black pepper. Add the parsley and stellette. Stir well.

Top each mushroom with the pasta mixture then place the baking sheet under a hot grill for 2–5 minutes, or until the topping is lightly golden and the mushrooms are warmed through.

Tagliatelle with Mushrooms

A quick supper for any occasion. Try using spaghetti or linguini for a change.

SERVES 4

450g/1lb dried tagliatelle

dash of olive oil

25g/1oz butter

1 clove of garlic, crushed

2tbsp chopped fresh parsley

225g/8oz button or cup mushrooms, sliced

salt and freshly ground black pepper

275ml/½pt single cream

freshly grated Parmesan cheese, to serve

Bring a large saucepan of water to the boil and add the tagliatelle with a dash of olive oil. Cook for about 10 minutes, stirring occasionally, until tender. Drain and set aside.

Meanwhile, melt the butter in a large frying pan and sauté the garlic and chopped parsley for 2–3 minutes. Add the sliced mushrooms and cook for 5–8 minutes, or until softened and slightly browned.

Season the mushroom mixture with salt and freshly ground black pepper, then stir in the cream. Cook the sauce for 1–2 minutes, then stir in the tagliatelle. Continue to cook while stirring to coat the tagliatelle in the sauce. Serve with plenty of freshly grated Parmesan cheese.

OPPOSITE *Pasta-topped Mushrooms*

CEP

Fusilli with Wild Mushrooms

Wild mushrooms, or ceps, are increasingly available and are the special ingredient in this dish. Dried ceps can be found in Italian delicatessens; they need to be soaked in water for 30 minutes before using in the recipe.

SERVES 4

325g/11oz dried long fusilli (twists)

dash of olive oil plus 75ml/5tbsp

1 clove of garlic, crushed

2tbsp chopped fresh thyme

150g/5oz fresh shiitake mushrooms, sliced

150g/5oz fresh oyster mushrooms

15g/½oz dried ceps, soaked, drained and sliced

salt and freshly ground black pepper

freshly grated Parmesan cheese, to serve

Bring a large saucepan of water to the boil and add the fusilli with a dash of olive oil. Cook for about 10 minutes, stirring occasionally, until tender. Drain and set aside, covered.

Heat the olive oil in a large frying pan and add the garlic and fresh thyme. Cook for 1–2 minutes, then stir in all the mushrooms and season to taste with salt and freshly ground black pepper.

Fry the mushroom mixture over high heat for 3–4 minutes to brown slightly, then turn the mixture into the saucepan containing the fusilli. Toss together briefly, then serve with a little freshly grated Parmesan cheese.

FIELD

Cheesy Mushroom Canapés

These tasty morsels are ideal for entertaining. They can be made in advance and are delicious served with drinks.

CONCHIGLIE

SERVES 8–10

20 dried large lumache rigate or large shells

dash of olive oil

3tbsp freshly grated Parmesan cheese

FOR THE FILLING:

30ml/2tbsp olive oil

1 clove of garlic, chopped

1 small onion, finely chopped

3tbsp chopped fresh parsley

175g/6oz button mushrooms, very finely chopped

50g/2oz pitted olives, very finely chopped

225g/8oz full-fat soft cheese

salt and freshly ground black pepper

Bring a large saucepan of water to the boil and add the pasta with a dash of olive oil. Cook for about 10 minutes, stirring occasionally, until tender. Drain and rinse under cold running water. Pat dry with absorbent kitchen paper and set aside.

To make the filling, heat the oil in a large frying pan and sauté the garlic and onion for about 3 minutes, until softened. Remove from the heat and stir in the remaining filling ingredients.

Use a teaspoon to stuff each pasta shape with the filling and arrange them on a baking sheet. Sprinkle with grated Parmesan cheese and place under a hot grill for about 5 minutes until golden. Arrange on a serving plate.

Creamy Mushroom Pasta Pie

A dish that is perfect for a romantic dinner for two. It can be made in advance and simply reheated to serve, so that you won't be tied to the kitchen.

SERVES 2

450g/1lb puff pastry, thawed if frozen

milk, to glaze

FOR THE FILLING:

175g/6oz dried wholewheat pasta shells

dash of olive oil

25g/1oz butter

1 clove of garlic, crushed

150g/5oz button mushrooms, sliced

75g/3oz baby sweetcorn, cut into chunks

40g/1½oz plain flour

150ml/¼pt milk

salt and freshly ground black pepper

50g/2oz mature Cheddar cheese

chopped fresh parsley, to garnish

Preheat the oven to 200°C/400°F/Gas Mark 6. Roll the pastry out into two rectangular pieces, each measuring 15 × 10cm/6 × 4inches. Set one rectangle aside to make the base of the pastry case. Take the other piece and cut out an inner rectangle using a ruler and a sharp knife, leaving a 2.5cm/1inch border to make the rim of the pastry case. Reserve the inner rectangle to make the lid and, using a sharp knife, score it to make a pattern. Brush a little milk around the edges of the base of the pastry case and place the rim in position on top.

Place on a baking sheet with the lid alongside and brush all the surfaces with a little milk to glaze. Bake for about 15–20 minutes, or until well-risen, and golden-brown. Remove from the oven and transfer it to a wire rack to cool. If the centre of the pastry case has risen too high, gently press down to create a hollow space. Place on a serving plate.

To make the filling, bring a large saucepan of water to the boil and add the wholewheat pasta shells with a dash of olive oil. Cook for about 10 minutes, stirring occasionally, until tender. Drain well and set aside.

Melt the butter in a large saucepan and sauté the garlic, mushrooms and baby sweetcorn for 5–8 minutes, or until softened. Stir in the flour and mix to form a paste. Gradually stir in the milk, a little at a time, stirring well after each addition. Bring the sauce slowly to the boil, stirring constantly to prevent lumps from forming. Season with salt and freshly ground black pepper. Stir in the grated cheese and continue to cook for a further 2–3 minutes, until the cheese has melted.

Stir the pasta in the sauce, then spoon the sauce into the pastry case. Sprinkle over the chopped fresh parsley, then place the lid on top and serve.

CONCHIGLIE

Mushroom Cannelloni

Cannelloni is a time-consuming dish to prepare, but it is always worth the effort. Cook more cannelloni pasta than is required to allow for any split ones.

SERVES 4

8 dried cannelloni

dash of olive oil

butter, for greasing

1 quantity Mushroom Sauce (page 9)

FOR THE FILLING:

30ml/2tbsp olive oil

1 clove of garlic, crushed

1 onion, finely chopped

3tsp chopped fresh thyme

225g/8oz button mushrooms, finely chopped

50g/2oz fine, fresh breadcrumbs

salt and freshly ground black pepper

Bring a large saucepan of water to the boil and add the cannelloni with a dash of olive oil. Cook for about 10 minutes, stirring occasionally, until tender. Drain and rinse under cold running water. Pat dry with absorbent kitchen paper and set aside.

To make the filling, heat the oil in a large frying pan and sauté the garlic, onion and thyme for about 3 minutes, or until the onion has softened.

Add the chopped mushrooms to the onion mixture and continue to cook for about 10 minutes, stirring frequently. Add the breadcrumbs and season with salt and freshly ground black pepper. Stir well.

Preheat the oven to 200°C/400°F/Gas Mark 6. Butter the inside of an ovenproof casserole dish. Using a teaspoon, stuff each cannelloni with the filling, then lay it in the casserole dish.

Pour the Mushroom Sauce evenly over the cannelloni then bake for about 30 minutes, until heated through and golden on top.

Mushroom Stroganoff with Pasta

A rich dinner-party dish that is delicious served with a glass of chilled dry white wine.

SERVES 4–6

50g/2oz butter

2 cloves of garlic, crushed

1 onion, sliced into thin wedges

675g/1½lb mixed mushrooms (oyster, maron, cup etc), left whole or cut in half

15g/½oz plain flour

150ml/¼pt vegetable stock

25ml/1floz dry white wine

salt and freshly ground black pepper

75ml/3floz double cream

3tbsp chopped fresh thyme

2tbsp ground paprika

675g/1½lb cooked tagliatelle, tossed in butter, to serve

Melt the butter in a large saucepan and sauté the garlic and onion for about 7 minutes, until the onion has browned slightly.

Add the mushrooms and cook for 2 minutes, then stir in the flour. Cook for 30 seconds, then gradually stir in the vegetable stock, then the wine. Bring the sauce to the boil and season with salt and freshly ground black pepper. Stir in the cream, fresh thyme and ground paprika. Cook for a further 2 minutes, then serve with hot buttered tagliatelle.

OYSTER

Deep-fried Mushroom Pasta Pockets

Serve this dish as a starter with a small dish of Garlic Mayonnaise (see Tip) for dipping.

SERVES 4–6

225g/8oz fresh lasagne

1 egg, beaten

sunflower oil, for deep-frying

FOR THE FILLING:

225g/8oz full-fat soft cheese with herbs and garlic

175g/6oz button mushrooms

Lay the fresh lasagne pasta out on the work surface and stamp out rounds using a 7.5cm/3inch cutter.

Place the full-fat soft cheese and the mushrooms in a food processor and blend to form a coarse texture.

Spoon some of the mushroom mixture on to one half of each pasta round. Brush a little of the beaten egg around the edges of the rounds then fold in half to encase the filling, sealing firmly with your fingers. Lay the mushroom pockets out on baking sheets and chill in the refrigerator for 30 minutes.

Heat the oil for deep frying and fry the mushroom pockets in batches for about 3 minutes, until crisp and golden. Remove from the oil and drain on absorbent kitchen paper. Place on a baking sheet and keep warm in a low oven until all the batches are cooked. Serve with Garlic Mayonnaise for dipping.

TIP:
To make Garlic Mayonnaise; mix 4 cloves of garlic, crushed, with 275ml/½pt mayonnaise. Chill for 30 minutes before serving.

Mushroom Stroganoff with Pasta.

Pinwheel Pasta Bake.

Pinwheel Pasta Bake

A homely dish that is perfect for a family supper. This is a good recipe for the freezer. When thawed, reheat, covered, in a medium-hot oven.

SERVES 4–6

675g/1½lb dried rotelle (pinwheels)

dash of olive oil

30ml/2tbsp sunflower oil

1 clove of garlic, crushed

225g/8oz mushrooms, quartered

100g/4oz courgettes, chopped

3tbsp chopped fresh parsley

150ml/¼pt vegetable stock

175g/6oz grated mature Cheddar cheese

Bring a large saucepan of water to the boil and add the rotelle with a dash of olive oil. Cook for about 10 minutes, sitrring occasionally, until tender. Drain and set aside.

Heat the sunflower oil in a large frying pan and sauté the garlic for 2 minutes. Add the mushrooms and courgettes and cook, covered, for 5 minutes, or until softened.

Stir the chopped parsley and vegetable stock into the mushroom mixture and continue to cook, covered, for a further 10 minutes. Add the rotelle and stir in the grated cheese.

Preheat the oven to 200°C/400°F/Gas Mark 6. Transfer the pasta mixture to a deep casserole dish and bake for about 20 minutes. Serve with warm crusty bread.

ROTELLE

Hearty Cream of Mushroom Soup

Perfect for a cold winter's night or even a filling lunchtime dish. Serve with warm, crusty garlic bread for a more substantial meal.

SERVES 4

25g/1oz butter

1 onion, finely chopped

350g/12oz cup mushrooms, finely chopped

1tbsp plain flour

575ml/1pt vegetable stock

275ml/½pt milk

salt and freshly ground black pepper

100g/4oz cooked tiny pasta shapes

pinch of freshly grated nutmeg

Melt the butter in a large saucepan and sauté the onion for about 3 minutes until softened. Add the chopped mushrooms, cover and cook for a further 5 minutes.

Stir in the flour, then gradually add the stock and milk, stirring well after each addition. Cover and cook for 15–20 minutes, stirring occasionally. Season with salt and freshly ground black pepper. Stir in the pasta shapes and grated nutmeg. Cook for a final 2–3 minutes, then serve.

Mushroom Ravioli

Once you have tasted
fresh, home-made ravioli
not only will you never buy
it ready-made again but
you will probably want to
invest in a ravioli pan,
which will make future
ravioli-making even easier.

SERVES 6

⅔ quantity Pasta Dough (page 8)

1 quantity Mushroom Sauce (page 9)

1 egg, beaten, for brushing

dash of olive oil

chopped fresh parsley, to garnish

freshly grated Parmesan cheese, to serve

FOR THE FILLING:

30ml/2tbsp olive oil

1 clove of garlic, crushed

3tbsp chopped fresh thyme

225g/8oz button mushrooms,
finely chopped

100g/4oz fine, fresh white breadcrumbs

salt and freshly ground black pepper

Keep the fresh pasta dough covered in clingfilm at room temperature and the Mushroom Sauce in a saucepan, ready to reheat later.

To make the filling, heat the oil in a large frying pan and add the garlic and fresh thyme. Cook for 1–2 minutes, then stir in the mushrooms and fry for 3–5 minutes. Stir in the breadcrumbs and season to taste with salt and freshly ground black pepper.

Remove from the heat and allow to cool completely.

To make the ravioli, cut the pasta dough in half. Roll out one half to a rectangle slightly larger than 35 × 25cm/14 × 10inches. Trim the edges of the dough neatly. Cover the rectangle with clingfilm to prevent it drying out. Roll out the other half of the dough to the same measurements. Do not trim the edges.

Place half teaspoonfuls of the filling mixture in lines, spaced about 2cm/¾inch apart, all over the trimmed rectangle of pasta dough. Brush the beaten egg lightly in lines around the filling mixture to make the square shapes for the ravioli.

Lay the other rectangle of pasta dough on top and, starting at one end, seal in the filling by lightly pressing the dough, pushing out any trapped air and gently flattening the filling, to make little packets. Using a sharp knife or a pastry wheel, cut down and across in lines around the filling to make the square ravioli.

To cook the ravioli, bring a large saucepan of water to the boil and add the ravioli with a dash of olive oil. Cook for about 6 minutes, stirring occasionally, until tender. Drain.

Meanwhile, reheat the Mushroom Sauce. Serve the Mushroom Ravioli with the Mushroom Sauce, sprinkled with chopped parsley and grated Parmesan cheese.

2 **Pasta** *with Tomatoes*

Bucatini with Tomatoes

This is a vegetarian version of a simple yet classic Italian dish. Use Parmesan cheese if Pecorino is not available.

SERVES 4

SERVES 4

350g/12oz dried bucatini (long tubes)

dash of olive oil

2 cloves of garlic, crushed

1 onion, finely chopped

450g/1lb carton sieved tomatoes

4tbsp chopped fresh basil

salt and freshly ground black pepper

butter, for greasing

50g/2oz freshly grated Pecorino or Parmesan cheese

YELLOW CHERRY

Bring a large saucepan of water to the boil and add the bucatini with a dash of olive oil. Cook for about 10 minutes, stirring occasionally, until tender. Drain and set aside.

Preheat the oven to 200°C/400°F/Gas Mark 6. Place the garlic, onion, sieved tomatoes, basil and salt and freshly ground black pepper in a large frying pan and heat until simmering. Cook for about 5 minutes, then remove from the heat.

Arrange the bucatini in a shallow, buttered ovenproof dish. Curl it round to fit the dish, adding one or two tubes at a time, until the dish is tightly packed with the pasta.

Spoon over the tomato mixture, prodding and poking the pasta to ensure the sauce sinks down to the bottom of the dish. Sprinkle the grated cheese over the top and bake for 25–30 minutes, until bubbling, crisp and golden. Cut in wedges, like a cake, to serve.

Tagliatelle Neapolitan

Yellow tomatoes make this dish look particularly attractive, though red ones taste just as good. If you can't find fresh tagliatelle, use the dried egg version.

SERVES 4

450g/1lb fresh multi-coloured tagliatelle

dash of olive oil, plus 30ml/2tbsp

2 cloves of garlic, crushed

1 onion, chopped

3tbsp chopped fresh basil or oregano

450g/1lb yellow and red tomatoes, skinned, seeded and chopped

225g/8oz carton sieved tomatoes

salt and freshly ground black pepper

fresh basil, to garnish

freshly grated Parmesan cheese, to serve

Bring a large saucepan of water to the boil and add the tagliatelle with a dash of olive oil. Cook for about 5 minutes, stirring occasionally, until tender. Drain and set aside, covered.

Heat the remaining oil in a large frying pan and sauté the garlic, onion and basil or oregano for about 3 minutes, or until the onion has softened.

Add the chopped tomato flesh and sieved tomatoes and season with salt and freshly ground black pepper. Stir and cook for about 10 minutes, until thickened and bubbling. Serve with the tagliatelle. Garnish with fresh basil and sprinkle with freshly grated Parmesan cheese.

Tomato Tortellini with Tomato Basil Sauce

Although fresh tortellini is increasingly available in supermarkets and delicatessens, nothing tastes quite as good as real home-made pasta. Once the production line is assembled, with the pasta shapes cut out and the filling on standby, the process is simple, efficient and fun!

TORTELLINI

SERVES 6–8

⅔ quantity Pasta Dough (page 8) with 15ml/1tbsp tomato purée beaten into the eggs

1 egg, beaten for brushing

dash of olive oil

chopped fresh basil, to garnish

freshly grated Parmesan cheese, to serve

FOR THE FILLING:

400g/14oz can chopped tomatoes, drained

2 cloves of garlic, crushed

175g/6oz fresh breadcrumbs

3tbsp chopped fresh basil

salt and freshly ground black pepper

FOR THE SAUCE:

30ml/2tbsp olive oil

1 clove of garlic, crushed

1 small onion, very finely chopped

400g/14oz can chopped tomatoes

30ml/2tbsp tomato purée

4tbsp chopped fresh basil

salt and freshly ground black pepper

Wrap the pasta dough in clingfilm to prevent it from drying out and set aside.

To make the filling, mix all the ingredients together in a medium-sized bowl and set aside, covered.

To make the sauce, heat the olive oil in a large saucepan and sauté the garlic and onion for about 5 minutes, until softened. Add the remaining sauce ingredients and simmer for 10–15 minutes, until bubbling and thickened. Set aside, covered, to keep warm.

To make the Tortellini, cut the pasta dough in half. Keep one portion covered with clingfilm and roll out the other portion to a 30cm/12inch square. Cut the dough into six 5cm/2inch strips. Now cut the strips into 5cm/2inch squares and brush each one with a little beaten egg.

Place a little of the tomato filling on each pasta square, then fold the squares over into triangles. Seal the edges, then wrap the long side of the triangle around the tip of your forefinger and pinch the corners together tightly. Continue sealing and shaping the tortellini, then roll out the other half of the pasta dough and repeat the process. Place the filled tortellini on baking sheets lined with greaseproof paper.

To cook the tortellini, bring a large saucepan of water to the boil and add the pasta with a dash of olive oil. Cook for about 5 minutes, stirring occasionally, until tender. Drain and set aside, covered, to keep warm.

Reheat the sauce and serve with the tortellini, garnished with chopped fresh basil and sprinkled with freshly grated Parmesan cheese.

TIP:
Do not overfill the tortellini with stuffing or they may split during cooking.

Fusilli with Sun-dried Tomatoes

A dish that is delicious served warm as a main course or cold as a summer salad. Tomato pesto is widely available.

SERVES 2–4

450g/1lb dried fusilli (twists)

dash of olive oil, plus extra for drizzling

30ml/2tbsp tomato pesto

175g/6oz sun-dried tomatoes, drained and chopped

4 plum tomatoes, sliced into wedges

4tbsp chopped fresh basil

salt and freshly ground black pepper

Bring a large saucepan of water to the boil and add the fusilli with a dash of olive oil. Cook for about 10 minutes, stirring occasionally, until tender. Drain and return to the saucepan.

Stir in the remaining ingredients, drizzle with olive oil and serve warm immediately, or cool and refrigerate to serve chilled if preferred.

OPPOSITE *Fusilli with Sun-dried Tomatoes.*

Spicy Stuffed Tomatoes

Beefsteak tomatoes are perfect for stuffing. Serve as a vegetable accompaniment or as a starter. To make the tomatoes stand up in the dish, slice a thin shaving off the bottom of each one.

SERVES 4

100g/4oz dried pastina (any tiny shapes)

dash of olive oil

4 large beefsteak tomatoes

butter, for greasing

FOR THE FILLING:

350g/12oz potatoes, cut into 5mm/¼inch cubes

60ml/4tbsp olive oil

2 cloves of garlic, crushed

1 onion, finely chopped

2tsp mild curry powder

pinch of ground cumin

15ml/1tbsp tomato purée

4tbsp chopped fresh coriander

salt and freshly ground black pepper

Bring a saucepan of water to the boil and add the pastina with a dash of olive oil. Cook for about 8 minutes, stirring occasionally, until tender. Drain and set aside.

Slice the tops off the tomatoes and reserve for the lids. Using a teaspoon, scrape out the flesh of each tomato and reserve. Arrange the hollowed tomatoes in a buttered oven-proof dish and set aside.

To make the filling, cook the potatoes in boiling water for about 10 minutes, until tender. Drain and set aside. Heat the olive oil in a large frying pan and sauté the garlic and onion for about 3 minutes, until softened.

Add the curry powder, cumin and tomato purée. Cook for 2 minutes, then gently stir in the pastina and cooked potato. Add the chopped coriander and season with salt and freshly ground black pepper. Cook for a further 2–3 minutes, stirring occasionally, then remove from the heat.

Preheat the oven to 200°C/400°F/Gas Mark 6. Stuff the tomatoes with the filling, placing any extra in the bottom of the dish. Place the tomato lids on top and bake for about 20 minutes, or until heated through.

BEEFSTEAK

Italian Spaghettini

Italian Spaghettini

Pine nuts give this dish its special taste and texture. Serve it straight from the pan.

PLUM

SERVES 4

450g/1lb dried multi-coloured spaghettini

dash of olive oil

50g/2oz butter

1 clove of garlic, crushed

1 small onion, very finely chopped

75g/3oz pine nuts

225g/8oz carton sieved tomatoes

salt and freshly ground black pepper

4tbsp chopped fresh basil

2tbsp chopped fresh parsley

Bring a large saucepan of water to the boil and add the dried spaghettini with a dash of olive oil. Cook for about 10 minutes, stirring occasionally, until tender. Drain and set aside.

Melt the butter in a large frying pan and sauté the garlic and onion for about 3 minutes, or until the onion has softened. Add the pine nuts and stir-fry until evenly golden.

Add the sieved tomatoes, salt and freshly ground black pepper and herbs and cook for about 5 minutes, stirring occasionally.

Add the spaghettini and stir well to coat in the tomato sauce. Cook for a further 5 minutes, then serve immediately.

Fettuccine with Tomatoes and Mozzarella

This delicious summertime salad can be made well in advance and left to marinate for up to 3 hours.

SERVES 4

350g/12oz dried egg fettuccine

dash of olive oil

450g/1lb beefsteak tomatoes, skinned, seeded and sliced

75ml/5tbsp extra virgin olive oil

2 cloves of garlic, crushed

6tbsp chopped fresh basil

2tbsp chopped fresh oregano

350g/12oz mozzarella cheese, cut into 1cm/½inch cubes

50g/2oz freshly grated Pecorino or Parmesan cheese

salt and freshly ground black pepper

Bring a large saucepan of water to the boil and add the fettuccine with a dash of olive oil. Cook for about 10 minutes, stirring occasionally, until tender. Drain and rinse under cold running water. Drain again and set aside.

In a large bowl, combine the sliced tomato flesh with the remaining ingredients and toss together lightly. Add the cooked fettuccine and mix lightly to coat in the oil. Serve this salad at room temperature with warm garlic bread.

Pasta al Pomodoro

Any pasta shapes would be suitable for this recipe, so use whatever you have in the cupboard. The sauce is quick and simple, making this dish a perfect supper for unexpected guests.

STELLETTI

SERVES 4–6

450g/1lb dried pasta

dash of olive oil

25g/1oz butter

2 cloves of garlic, crushed

1 onion, chopped

450g/1lb carton sieved tomatoes

salt and freshly ground black pepper

fresh flat parsley sprigs, to garnish

slivers of fresh Parmesan cheese, to serve

Bring a saucepan of water to the boil and add the pasta with a dash of olive oil. Cook for about 10 minutes, stirring occasionally, until tender. Drain and set aside, covered, to keep warm.

Melt the butter in a large frying pan and sauté the garlic and onion for about 3 minutes, until softened. Stir in the tomatoes and season with salt and freshly ground black pepper. Simmer the sauce for about 10 minutes then serve with the pasta, garnished with parsley sprigs and sprinkled with slivers of fresh Parmesan cheese.

> **TIP:**
> To make slivers of Parmesan cheese, use a vegetable peeler.

Tomato Vegetable Crumble

A delicious, wholesome main-course dish. Serve with lightly cooked green beans tossed in butter and black pepper.

PLUM

SERVES 4–6

450g/1lb dried macaroni

dash of olive oil, plus 30ml/2tbsp

2 cloves of garlic, crushed

1 onion, chopped

4tbsp chopped fresh parsley

400g/14oz can chopped tomatoes

100g/4oz tomatoes, chopped

30ml/2tbsp tomato purée

salt and freshly ground black pepper

FOR THE TOPPING:

175g/6oz rolled oats

75g/3oz ground hazelnuts

50g/2oz freshly grated Parmesan cheese

3tsp dried thyme

75g/3oz butter

Bring a large saucepan of water to the boil and add the macaroni with a dash of olive oil. Cook for about 10 minutes, stirring occasionally, until tender. Drain and set aside.

Heat the remaining olive oil in a large frying pan and sauté the garlic and onion for about 3 minutes, until softened. Add the parsley, chopped tomatoes, tomato purée and salt and freshly ground black pepper. Cook for about 5 minutes, then stir in the macaroni. Turn the macaroni mixture into a shallow ovenproof dish and set aside. Preheat the oven to 180°C/350°F/Gas Mark 4.

To make the topping, combine all the ingredients in a mixing bowl and rub in the butter until the mixture resembles bread-crumbs. Scatter the topping over the tomato macaroni and press down gently. Bake for about 30 minutes, until golden and heated through.

Macaroni Neapolitan

A quick and delicious way to serve macaroni. Serve with a crisp green salad. Ring the changes by using a different pasta shape for this dish each time you make it.

SERVES 4

450g/1lb dried macaroni

dash of olive oil, plus 90ml/6tbsp

2 cloves of garlic, crushed

4tbsp chopped fresh parsley

2 × 450g/1lb cartons pulped tomatoes

15ml/1tbsp tomato purée

salt and freshly ground black pepper

25g/1oz freshly grated Parmesan cheese

Bring a large saucepan of water to the boil and add the macaroni with a dash of olive oil. Cook for about 10 minutes, stirring occasionally, until tender. Drain and return to the saucepan to keep warm.

Preheat the oven to 200°C/400°F/Gas Mark 6. Heat the remaining oil in a large frying pan and sauté the garlic with the parsley for 2–3 minutes, stirring frequently. Add the tomatoes, tomato purée and salt and freshly ground black pepper. Cook for about 10 minutes, stirring occasionally.

Stir the tomato sauce evenly into the macaroni, then transfer the mixture to an ovenproof dish. Sprinkle the Parmesan cheese over the top and bake for about 30 minutes.

Tomato Pasta Timbales

An attractive first course, these timbales are very easy to make and are sure to impress your guests. Make them up to one hour in advance and place them in the oven to bake.

BEEFSTEAK

SERVES 4

350g/12oz dried multi-coloured spaghettini

dash of olive oil, plus extra for greasing

4 small tomato slices

30ml/2tbsp tomato pesto

2 eggs, beaten

50ml/2floz milk

salt and freshly ground black pepper

FOR THE SAUCE:

225g/8oz carton sieved tomatoes

15ml/1tbsp sweet soya sauce

4tbsp chopped fresh basil

salt and freshly ground black pepper

TO GARNISH:

fresh flat parsley sprigs

cherry tomatoes

Bring a large saucepan of water to the boil and add the spaghettini with a dash of olive oil. Cook for about 10 minutes, stirring occasionally, until tender. Drain well.

Preheat the oven to 160°C/325°F/Gas Mark 3. Grease four 175ml/6floz individual ovenproof moulds with a little olive oil and place a circle of greaseproof paper in the bottom of each. Place a slice of tomato in the base of each mould then carefully pack in the spaghettini, leaving a 6mm/¼inch space at the top.

In a mixing jug, combine the tomato pesto, eggs, milk and salt and freshly ground black pepper. Beat well then pour into each spaghettini mould, covering the pasta.

Arrange the moulds in a roasting pan with enough boiling water to come halfway up the sides. Bake for about 40 minutes, until set and firm to the touch.

Meanwhile, to make the sauce, place all the ingredients in a saucepan and heat to simmering point. Simmer for 10 minutes, until thickened slightly.

Run a sharp knife around the edges of each timbale, then invert each on to individual plates. Pour a little sauce around each timbale and garnish.

Tomato and Pasta Salad

Orecchiette are small ear-shaped pasta. If they are not available, gnocchi pasta shapes (dumplings) will work just as well.

CONCHIGLIE

SERVES 6–8

550g/1¼lb fresh orecchiette (ears)

dash of olive oil

450g/1lb red and yellow tomatoes, chopped

15cm/6inch piece cucumber, chopped

175g/6oz feta cheese, chopped

5tbsp chopped fresh coriander

2tbsp chopped fresh basil

FOR THE DRESSING:

15ml/1tbsp white wine vinegar

60ml/4tbsp olive oil

2 cloves of garlic, crushed

salt and freshly ground black pepper

TO GARNISH:

cherry tomatoes

fresh coriander sprigs

Bring a large saucepan of water to the boil and add the orecchiette with a dash of olive oil. Cook for about 5 minutes, stirring occasionally, until tender. Drain and rinse under cold running water. Drain again and set aside.

Place the orecchiette in a large mixing bowl and add the remaining salad ingredients. Mix to combine. To make the dressing, place all the ingredients in a screw-top jar and shake well. Pour the dressing over the salad and toss to coat. Serve garnished with cherry tomatoes and coriander sprigs.

Tomato Mozzarella Kebabs

These are excellent for a vegetarian barbecue. Serve the kebabs with plenty of hot, crusty garlic bread and salad.

SERVES 4

100g/4oz dried rotelle (pinwheels)

dash of olive oil, plus 60ml/4tbsp

2 cloves of garlic, crushed

salt and freshly ground black pepper

8–12 cherry tomatoes

225g/8oz mozzarella cheese, cut into 2.5cm/1inch cubes

Bring a large saucepan of water to the boil and add the rotelle with a dash of olive oil. Cook for about 10 minutes, stirring occasionally, until tender. Drain and rinse under cold running water. Drain again and set aside.

In a small bowl, combine the olive oil, garlic and salt and freshly ground black pepper. Set aside.

YELLOW CHERRY

To make the kebabs, place one rotelle, a tomato, then a cube of mozzarella cheese on to kebab skewers until all the ingredients have been used. Arrange the skewers on a baking sheet and brush liberally with the garlic olive oil mixture, turning the kebabs to coat evenly.

Place the kebabs under a preheated grill for 5–7 minutes, turning the skewers halfway through cooking, until browned. Serve immediately.

> **TIP:**
> If using wooden skewers, soak them for at least one hour in water before threading on the kebab ingredients. This will help prevent them from burning during grilling.

Spaghettini with Tomato Ragout

This version of ragout is a brilliant standby sauce to use when hunger won't wait for time.

SERVES 4

450g/1lb dried spaghettini

dash of olive oil

freshly grated Parmesan cheese, to serve

FOR THE RAGOUT:

25g/1oz butter

1 clove of garlic, crushed

1 large onion, finely chopped

400g/14oz can chopped tomatoes

150ml/¼pt dry red wine

4tbsp chopped fresh basil

salt and freshly ground black pepper

Bring a large saucepan of water to the boil and add the spaghettini with a dash of olive oil. Cook for about 10 minutes, stirring occasionally, until tender. Drain and set aside, covered, to keep warm.

To make the ragout, melt the butter in a large frying pan and sauté the garlic and onion for about 3 minutes, until softened. Add the remaining ragout ingredients, stir and simmer for 15 minutes, until slightly thickened. Serve with the spaghettini, sprinkled with freshly grated Parmesan cheese.

OPPOSITE *Tomato Mozzarella Kebabs.*

Trenette with Tomato Tarragon Cream

This is a rich pasta dish which is not for the health conscious! However, it is extremely delicious with a glass of chilled dry white wine.

SERVES 4

450g/1lb dried trenette (long, wavy strips)

dash of olive oil, plus 15ml/1tbsp

2 cloves of garlic, crushed

4tbsp chopped fresh tarragon

225g/8oz cherry tomatoes, halved

275ml/½pt single cream

salt and freshly ground black pepper

freshly grated Parmesan cheese, to serve

Bring a large saucepan of water to the boil and add the trenette with a dash of olive oil. Cook for about 10 minutes, stirring occasionally, until tender. Drain and return to the saucepan. Set aside, covered, to keep warm.

Heat the remaining olive oil in a large frying pan and add the garlic, tarragon and tomatoes. Sauté for about 3 minutes, stirring occasionally, then stir in the cream. Season with salt and freshly ground black pepper and cook for 2–3 minutes, until heated through. Stir into the pasta, then serve with freshly grated Parmesan cheese.

3 **Pasta** *with Peppers*

Stuffed Peppers

A refreshing alternative to rice, pasta makes a perfect filling for peppers. Tiny pasta shapes also work well in this dish. Serve with a crisp green salad.

SERVES 4

225g/8oz gnocchetti sardi (small dumpling shapes)

dash of olive oil

4 peppers, for stuffing

flat leaf parsley sprigs, to garnish

FOR THE FILLING:

50g/2oz butter

6 spring onions, finely chopped

2 cloves of garlic, crushed

1 pepper, seeded and finely diced

salt and freshly ground black pepper

50g/2oz freshly grated Parmesan cheese

Bring a large saucepan of water to the boil and add the gnocchetti sardi with a dash of olive oil. Cook for about 10 minutes, stirring occasionally, until tender. Drain and set aside.

Preheat the oven to 200°C/400°F/Gas Mark 6. Lay each pepper on its side and slice off the top, reserving it to make the lid. Scoop out the seeds and pith and discard. Arrange the hollowed-out peppers in a shallow ovenproof dish and set aside.

To make the filling, melt the butter in a large frying pan and sauté the spring onions and garlic for about 2 minutes, then add the diced pepper. Season with salt and freshly ground black pepper and cook for about 5 minutes, stirring occasionally.

Add the gnocchetti and the Parmesan cheese to the filling mixture and cook for about 2 minutes to heat through. Using a dessertspoon, stuff each pepper with the pasta filling, scattering any extra around the edges.

Place the pepper lids in the dish and bake for about 30 minutes, until the peppers have softened. Place under a hot grill for 2–3 minutes, if wished, just before serving, to char the pepper skins. Serve garnished with parsley sprigs.

RED

Pepper and Pasta Ratatouille.

Pepper and Pasta Ratatouille

Delicious served with a hot, buttered baked potato, this dish makes perfect bonfire-night fare.

CONCHIGLIE

SERVES 4–6

450g/1lb dried wholewheat gnocchi piccoli (small shells)

dash of olive oil, plus 45ml/3tbsp

2 cloves of garlic, crushed

1 onion, chopped

2 green peppers, seeded and cut into chunks

400g/14oz can chopped tomatoes

50g/2oz tomato purée

150ml/¼pt dry red wine

2tbsp fresh oregano

salt and freshly ground black pepper

fresh oregano sprigs, to garnish

Bring a large saucepan of water to the boil and add the gnocchi piccoli with a dash of olive oil. Cook for about 10 minutes, stirring occasionally, until tender. Drain and set aside.

Heat the remaining olive oil in a large saucepan and sauté the garlic and onion for about 3 minutes, until softened. Stir in the pepper chunks. Cover and cook for about 5 minutes, or until the pepper has softened slightly.

Stir in the remaining ingredients, except the oregano sprigs, into the pepper mixture and bring to simmering point. Reduce the heat, cover and cook for about 10 minutes, then stir in the gnocchi piccoli. Cook for a further 5 minutes, stirring occasionally. Serve garnished with fresh oregano sprigs.

Pasta with Pepper Sauce and Olives

This low-fat Pepper Sauce helps to keep the calories in this dish down. As long as the pasta used is dairy-free, this dish is also suitable for vegans.

SERVES 4

375g/13oz dried rigatoni (short tubes)

dash of olive oil

50g/2oz stoned black olives, roughly chopped

grated Cheddar cheese, to serve

FOR THE PEPPER SAUCE:

2 red peppers, skinned, seeded and roughly chopped

4 cloves of garlic, peeled

275g/½pt vegetable stock

salt and freshly ground black pepper

Bring a large saucepan of water to the boil and add the rigatoni with a dash of olive oil. Cook for about 10 minutes, stirring occasionally, until tender. Drain and return to the saucepan. Set aside.

To make the sauce, place the chopped pepper, garlic and vegetable stock in a food processor or blender and season with salt and freshly ground black pepper. Purée until smooth.

Stir the Pepper Sauce into the rigatoni with the chopped olives. Serve with grated Cheddar cheese.

Tortellini, Peppers and Pine Nut Salad

Red peppers can be used instead of chilli peppers, if you prefer. For best results allow the salad to chill for at least an hour before serving.

SERVES 4–6

275g/10oz fresh tortellini

dash of olive oil

1 onion, very finely sliced

1 green pepper, seeded and very finely diced

75g/3oz toasted pine nuts

1 red chilli pepper, seeded and sliced (optional)

10cm/4inch piece of cucumber, very thinly sliced

1 orange, peeled and very thinly sliced

FOR THE DRESSING:

60ml/4tbsp olive oil

30ml/2tbsp sweet soya sauce

30ml/2tbsp vinegar

salt and freshly ground black pepper

Bring a large saucepan of water to the boil and add the tortellini with a dash of olive oil. Cook for about 4 minutes, stirring occasionally, until tender. Drain and rinse under cold running water. Drain again and set aside.

Place the tortellini in a large mixing bowl and add the remaining salad ingredients. Toss together lightly.

To make the salad dressing, place the ingredients in a screw-top jar and shake well to combine. Pour the dressing over the salad, toss and serve.

CHILLIES

Rigatoni with Peppers and Garlic

The raw garlic added at the end of the recipe gives this dish the true taste of the Mediterranean.

YELLOW

SERVES 4

350g/12oz dried rigatoni (large tubes)

dash of olive oil, plus 60ml/4tbsp

1 large onion, chopped

4 cloves of garlic, finely chopped

2 large red peppers, seeded and roughly chopped

2 large yellow peppers, seeded and roughly chopped

2tsp chopped fresh thyme

salt and freshly ground black pepper

Bring a large saucepan of water to the boil and add the rigatoni with a dash of olive oil. Cook for about 10 minutes, stirring occasionally, until tender. Drain and set aside.

Heat the remaining oil in a large frying pan. Add the onion, 2 cloves of garlic, peppers and thyme. Cook over a medium heat for 10–15 minutes, stirring occasionally, until the vegetables are tender and beginning to brown.

Add the pasta shapes to the pepper mixture. Stir in the remaining garlic and seasoning. Serve immediately.

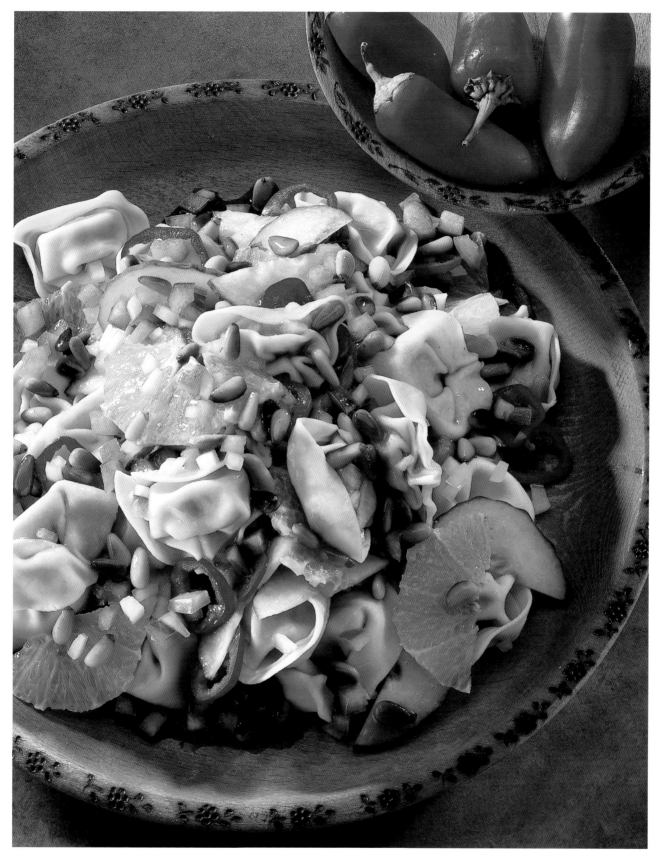

Tortellini, Peppers and Pine Nut Salad.

Pimiento Pasta

A quick store-cupboard

recipe for a last-minute

supper surprise.

SERVES 4

350g/12oz dried spaghettini

dash of olive oil, plus 30ml/2tbsp

2 cloves of garlic, crushed

400g/14oz can red pimiento, thinly sliced

salt and freshly ground black pepper

freshly grated Parmesan cheese, to serve
(optional)

Bring a large saucepan of water to the boil and add the spaghettini with a dash of olive oil. Cook for about 10 minutes, stirring occasionally, until tender. Drain and return to the saucepan. Set aside, covered, to keep warm.

Heat the remaining olive oil in a frying pan and add the garlic and sliced pimiento. Stir-fry for 3–5 minutes, then tip into the warm spaghettini. Stir to combine. Serve with a little freshly grated Parmesan cheese, if wished.

Pasta with Green Peppers and Pesto

If linguini is unavailable, spaghettini or tagliatelle will work just as well in this dish.

TARRAGON

SERVES 4

450g/1lb fresh linguini (thin, flat strips)

dash of olive oil, plus 30ml/2tbsp

2 cloves of garlic, crushed

½ quantity Pesto Sauce (page 10)

50ml/2floz vegetable stock

1 green pepper, seeded and very thinly sliced

fresh herbs, to garnish

Bring a large saucepan of water to the boil and add the linguini with a dash of olive oil. Cook for about 4 minutes, stirring occasionally, until tender. Drain and return to the saucepan. Stir in a dash more olive oil and set aside, covered, to keep warm.

Heat the remaining olive oil in a large frying pan and sauté the garlic for 1–2 minutes, then stir in the Pesto Sauce. Add the vegetable stock, stir and cook for 1 minute, then add the pepper slices. Cook for a further 7–10 minutes, stirring occasionally, until the pepper has softened. Stir the pepper mixture into the linguini and serve, garnished with fresh herbs.

Minty Pepper Salad

Serve this cool, light and refreshing salad for a summer lunch, or make it for a picnic as it packs and travels well.

350g/12oz dried macaroni

dash of olive oil, plus extra for drizzling

1 yellow pepper, seeded and cut into
1cm/½inch diamonds

1 green pepper, seeded and cut into
1cm/½inch diamonds

400g/14oz can artichoke hearts, drained and
quartered

15cm/6inch piece of cucumber, sliced

handful of mint leaves

salt and freshly ground black pepper

100g/4oz freshly grated Parmesan cheese

Bring a large saucepan of water to the boil
and add the macaroni with a dash of olive
oil. Cook for about 10 minutes, stirring
occasionally, until tender. Drain and rinse
under cold running water. Drain again and
place in a large mixing bowl.

Add the remaining ingredients to the
pasta and mix well to combine. Drizzle over
some olive oil and serve.

YELLOW

Red Pepper Soup

A delicious, wholesome,

filling soup, served with

your favourite pasta

shapes.

SERVES 4

400g/14oz can pimiento, drained

575ml/1pt vegetable stock

salt and freshly ground black pepper

1tbsp ground coriander

225g/8oz pasta shapes, such as tortelloni, shells, bows etc, cooked

fresh coriander, to garnish

Place the pimiento in a food processor or blender and purée until smooth. Transfer to a large saucepan and add the vegetable stock, salt and pepper and ground coriander. Stir and cook over gentle heat for about 10 minutes. Add the cooked pasta shapes and cook for a further 2–3 minutes, until heated through. Serve garnished with fresh coriander.

Sweet and Sour Peppers

Quick and easy, this dish

makes an excellent starter

or main course, served

warm or cold.

SERVES 4–6

350g/12oz dried farfalle (bows)

dash of olive oil, plus 60ml/4tbsp

2 onions, sliced

2 cloves of garlic, crushed

675g/1½lb black peppers, seeded and cut into chunks

1 red pepper, seeded and cut into strips

25g/1oz soft brown sugar

25g/1oz raisins

juice of 2 lemons

150ml/¼pt vegetable stock

salt and freshly ground black pepper

chopped fresh parsley, to garnish

Bring a large saucepan of water to the boil and add the farfalle with a dash of olive oil. Cook for about 10 minutes, stirring occasionally, until tender. Drain and set aside.

Heat the remaining olive oil in a large frying pan and add the onion and garlic. Sauté for about 3 minutes, until the onion has softened.

Add the black and red peppers. Stir, cover and cook over gentle heat for about 10 minutes, stirring occasionally, until the peppers have softened.

Stir in the remaining ingredients and simmer, uncovered, for about 5 minutes, stirring occasionally, until the sauce has reduced slightly.

Add the cooked farfalle and stir well to combine. Serve sprinkled with chopped fresh parsley.

Red Pepper Soup

Fusilli with Roasted Peppers.

Fusilli with Roasted Peppers

To prevent the pasta from sticking together, wash off the starchy cooking liquid by rinsing the pasta under boiling water from the kettle. Continue as directed in the recipe.

SERVES 4–6

450g/1lb dried long fusilli

dash of olive oil

2 yellow peppers, seeded and cut into chunks

3 cloves of garlic, crushed

50ml/2floz olive oil

100g/4oz grated Cheddar cheese

50g/2oz freshly grated Parmesan cheese

chopped fresh parsley, to garnish

Bring a large saucepan of water to the boil and add the fusilli with a dash of olive oil. Cook for about 10 minutes, stirring occasionally, until tender. Drain, return to the saucepan and set aside.

Preheat the oven to 200°C/400°F/Gas Mark 6. Arrange the chunks of pepper on a baking sheet and place under a hot grill for about 5 minutes, or until slightly charred.

Mix the pepper into the pasta with the remaining ingredients and toss together to combine. Transfer to an ovenproof dish and bake for about 15 minutes, or until heated through and the cheese has melted. Sprinkle over the chopped parsley and serve.

Cheesy Pepper Supper

Based on a traditional macaroni cheese, this colourful, tasty supper is a great dish for kids.

SERVES 4–6

225g/8oz dried macaroni

1/2 red pepper, seeded and finely diced

1/2 yellow pepper, seeded and finely diced

dash of olive oil

FOR THE SAUCE:

50g/2oz butter

50g/2oz plain flour

575ml/1pt milk

10ml/2tsp French mustard

25g/1oz grated Cheddar cheese

salt and freshly ground black pepper

FOR THE TOPPING:

100g/4oz fresh breadcrumbs

50g/2oz grated Cheddar cheese

YELLOW

Bring a large saucepan of water to the boil and add the macaroni with the diced peppers and a dash of olive oil. Cook for about 10 minutes, stirring occasionally, until tender. Drain and transfer to a shallow ovenproof dish. Set aside. Preheat the oven to 200°C/400°F/Gas Mark 6.

To make the sauce, melt the butter in a large saucepan and stir in the flour to make a paste. Gradually stir in the milk, a little at a time, until evenly blended, with no lumps.

Gently bring the sauce to the boil, stirring constantly, until thickened. Stir in the mustard and cheese and season with salt and pepper. Continue to cook for a further 1–2 minutes, until the cheese has melted.

Pour the cheese sauce over the macaroni and pepper mixture and mix it in with a spoon. When the sauce and pasta are evenly combined, sprinkle over the topping ingredients and bake for 25–30 minutes, until crisp and golden.

Tri-coloured Purée with Pasta

A dinner-party dish which can be prepared the day before and kept in the fridge. Reheat the sauces just before serving.

SERVES 4–6

450g/1lb dried spaghetti

dash of olive oil

50g/2oz butter

100g/4oz freshly grated Parmesan cheese

salt and freshly ground black pepper

FOR THE SAUCES:

3 red peppers, seeded and chopped

2 green peppers, seeded and chopped

1 yellow pepper, seeded and chopped

825ml/1½pt vegetable stock

10ml/2tsp tomato purée

1tbsp chopped fresh parsley

½tsp ground turmeric

salt and freshly ground black pepper

Bring a large saucepan of water to the boil and add the spaghetti with a dash of olive oil. Cook for about 10 minutes, stirring occasionally, until tender. Drain and return to the saucepan. Stir in the butter and Parmesan cheese and season with salt and freshly ground black pepper. Cover to keep warm and set aside.

To make the sauces, place the red, green and yellow peppers in a large saucepan and cover with boiling water. Cook for about 10 minutes, then drain.

Purée each of the colours separately in a blender or food processor, washing out between colours. Place each colour of pepper purée in a mixing jug or bowl and stir in enough vegetable stock to make the red pepper sauce up to 575ml/1pt, the green pepper sauce up to 425ml/¾pt and the yellow pepper sauce up to 275ml/½pt.

Stir in the tomato purée into the red pepper sauce, the chopped parsley into the green pepper sauce and the ground turmeric into the yellow pepper sauce. Season all three sauces with salt and freshly ground black pepper.

Transfer the sauces into separate saucepans to reheat, if necessary, then serve with the cheesy spaghetti.

PARSLEY

Pepper Pasta Soufflé

Perfect for a romantic dinner for two. But remember, timing is crucial! Make sure all your guests are seated before removing the soufflé from the oven.

YELLOW

SERVES 2

100g/4oz fresh spinach tagliatelle

dash of olive oil, plus 30ml/2tbsp

1 clove of garlic, crushed

225g/8oz mixed coloured peppers, seeded and cut into thin strips

2tbsp chopped fresh oregano

FOR THE SOUFFLÉ:

40g/1½oz butter plus extra for greasing

20g/¾oz plain flour

325ml/12floz milk

25g/1oz freshly grated Parmesan cheese

4 eggs, separated

Bring a large saucepan of water to the boil and add the tagliatelle with a dash of olive oil. Cook for 3–5 minutes, stirring occasionally, until tender. Drain and roughly chop. Set aside.

Heat the remaining olive oil in a frying pan and add the garlic. Cook for 1–2 minutes, then stir in the pepper strips with the oregano. Cover and cook over gentle heat for about 10 minutes, stirring occasionally, until the peppers have softened. Remove from the heat and set aside. Preheat the oven to 200°C/400°F/Gas Mark 6.

To make the soufflé, butter two 425ml/ ¾pt soufflé dishes and set aside. Melt the butter in a saucepan and stir in the flour to make a paste. Gradually stir in the milk, then bring the sauce to the boil, stirring constantly to prevent lumps, until thickened.

Stir in the Parmesan cheese and beat in the egg yolks, one at a time. Stir in the chopped tagliatelle until evenly coated.

Whisk the egg whites in a clean, dry bowl until stiff. Fold the egg whites into the tagliatelle mixture, then divide between the prepared soufflé dishes. Spoon the pepper mixture on top of each soufflé then bake for 20–25 minutes until risen and golden. Serve immediately.

4 **Pasta** *with Brassicas*

Floret Soup

A pretty and delicately flavoured soup for a dinner-party menu. Make it in advance and reheat to serve.

SERVES 4–6

25g/1oz butter

2 cloves of garlic, crushed

350g/12oz tiny broccoli, cauliflower and romanesco florets

100g/4oz dried pastina (any tiny shapes)

1.1l/2pt vegetable stock

salt and freshly ground black pepper

Melt the butter in a large saucepan and sauté the garlic for about 2 minutes. Add the tiny florets to the garlic and cook for about 5 minutes, stirring occasionally, until tender.

Stir the pastina into the floret mixture, cook for 1–2 minutes, then add the vegetable stock. Season with salt and freshly ground black pepper, cover and bring to the boil. Simmer for about 10 minutes, until the pastina is cooked and the florets have softened. Serve with warm, fresh bread.

Baby Cauliflower and Broccoli Cheese

Baby vegetables can be both formal and fun. To make this recipe suitable for children, omit the wine and cream from the sauce.

BROCCOLI

350g/12oz dried casareccia (long curled shapes)

dash of olive oil

50g/2oz butter

salt and freshly ground black pepper

6 baby cauliflowers

6 baby broccoli spears

1 quantity Cheese Sauce (page 9)

45ml/3tbsp dry white wine

30ml/2tbsp double cream

75g/3oz grated mature Cheddar cheese

Bring a large saucepan of water to the boil and add the casareccia with a dash of olive oil. Cook for about 10 minutes, stirring occasionally, until tender. Drain and return to the saucepan with the butter and season with salt and freshly ground black pepper. Set aside, covered, to keep warm.

Bring a large saucepan of water to the boil and add the baby cauliflower and baby broccoli. Cook for about 5 minutes, until tender. Drain and return to the saucepan, covered, to keep warm.

Place the Cheese Sauce in a saucepan and stir in the wine and cream. Heat gently, stirring constantly, for about 5 minutes.

To serve, divide the pasta between four warmed individual plates and arrange the baby vegetables on top. Pour over the Cheese Sauce and sprinkle with grated cheese. Serve immediately.

Gnocchetti Sardi with Broccoli and Tomatoes

A lovely light lunch or supper dish. Choose vivid green, tightly packed heads of broccoli and cook as briefly as possible to retain the colour and crisp texture.

TARRAGON

SERVES 4

350g/12oz dried gnocchetti sardi (small dumpling shapes)

dash of olive oil

75g/3oz unsalted butter

350g/12oz small broccoli florets

1 clove of garlic, chopped

2tsp chopped fresh rosemary

2tsp chopped fresh oregano

salt and freshly ground black pepper

200g/7oz can chopped tomatoes

15ml/1tbsp tomato purée

fresh herbs, to garnish

Bring a large saucepan of water to the boil and add the gnocchetti sardi with a dash of olive oil. Cook for about 6 minutes, stirring occasionally, until tender. Drain and return to the saucepan, covered, to keep warm.

Meanwhile, melt the butter in a large frying pan. Add the broccoli, garlic, rosemary and oregano and season with salt and freshly ground black pepper. Cover and cook gently for about 5 minutes, until tender.

Add the chopped tomatoes and tomato purée and stir. Add the gnocchetti sardi, mix together lightly, then serve immediately, garnished with fresh herbs.

Buckwheat Noodles with Savoy Cabbage

Buckwheat noodles, known as "pizzoccheri", are a speciality of northern Italy, they are available from specialist delicatessens. Wholewheat or egg tagliatelle make good substitutes.

SERVES 6

350g/12oz dried buckwheat noodles

225g/8oz savoy cabbage, shredded

225g/8oz potatoes, peeled and diced

dash of olive oil

150g/5oz unsalted butter

2 cloves of garlic, chopped

4tbsp chopped fresh sage

pinch of freshly grated nutmeg

200g/7oz diced Fontina cheese

100g/4oz freshly grated Parmesan cheese

Bring a large saucepan of water to the boil and add the buckwheat noodles, cabbage and potatoes with a dash of olive oil. Cook for 10–15 minutes, stirring occasionally, until tender. Drain and set aside, covered, to keep warm.

Meanwhile, melt the butter in a large frying pan and sauté the garlic and sage for about 1 minute. Remove from the heat and set aside.

Place a layer of the pasta and vegetables in a warm serving dish and sprinkle with a little nutmeg, some of the Fontina cheese and some of the Parmesan cheese.

Repeat the layers, then pour over the hot garlic butter. Mix lightly into the pasta and serve immediately.

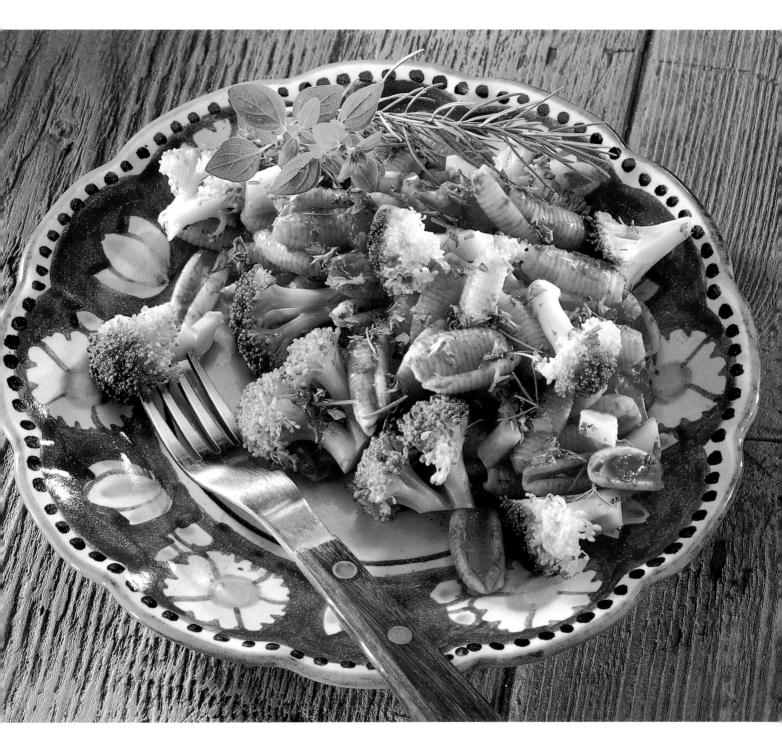

Gnocchetti Sardi with Broccoli and Tomatoes.

Braised Red Cabbage and Pasta Bake

A hearty supper dish for the family which is delicious served with creamed potatoes.

SERVES 4

225g/8oz dried ziti (short macaroni)	1tbsp chopped fresh thyme
dash of olive oil	450g/1lb red cabbage, chopped
50g/2oz butter	75g/3oz sultanas
1 onion, chopped	50g/2oz roasted pine nuts
2 cloves of garlic, crushed	salt and freshly ground black pepper
	175g/6oz grated mature Cheddar cheese

Bring a large saucepan of water to the boil and add the ziti with a dash of olive oil. Cook for about 10 minutes, stirring occasionally, until tender. Drain and set aside. Preheat the oven to 200°C/400°F/Gas Mark 6.

Melt the butter in a large frying pan and sauté the onion, garlic and thyme for about 3 minutes, until softened. Add the chopped red cabbage, sultanas and pine nuts and season to taste with salt and freshly ground black pepper. Cover and cook for 10 minutes, stirring occasionally, until the cabbage has softened.

Stir in the ziti then transfer the mixture to a shallow ovenproof dish. Top with the grated Cheddar cheese and bake for about 20 minutes, until golden. Serve immediately.

FUSILLI

Cheesy Cauliflower Crumble

A great way of serving vegetables as a main course. Serve this crumble with lightly cooked green beans and creamed potatoes for a really satisfying family supper.

SERVES 4

75g/3oz dried pastina (any tiny shapes)

dash of olive oil

900g/2lb cauliflower florets, trimmed

50g/2oz butter

salt and freshly ground black pepper

FOR THE TOPPING:

75g/3oz rolled oats

75g/3oz ground hazelnuts

75g/3oz ground almonds

1 small onion, very finely chopped

1 clove of garlic, crushed

1tsp dried thyme

salt and freshly ground black pepper

50g/2oz butter

50g/2oz grated mature Cheddar cheese

RED CABBAGE

Bring a large saucepan of water to the boil and add the pastina with a dash of olive oil. Cook for about 8 minutes, stirring occasionally, until tender. Drain and rinse under cold running water. Drain again.

Place the cauliflower florets in a large saucepan of boiling water and cook for 10–15 minutes, until tender. Drain, reserving the cooking water, and return to the saucepan. Place about a third of the cauliflower and 2oz butter in a food processor or blender with enough of the reserved cooking water to make a smooth purée. Stir the cauliflower purée into the remaining florets and season with salt and pepper. Transfer the cauliflower mixture to a shallow, ovenproof dish and set aside. Preheat the oven to 180°C/350°F/Gas Mark 4.

To make the topping, place the pastina in a mixing bowl with the rolled oats, ground nuts, onion, garlic and dried thyme. Season with salt and freshly ground black pepper and rub in 2oz butter until the mixture resembles coarse breadcrumbs.

Sprinkle the topping over the cauliflower mixture then scatter the grated cheese on top. Bake for about 35 minutes, until crisp and golden.

Cabbage and Pasta Mould.

Cabbage and Pasta Mould

Serve as an impressive dish for family or friends. Quick and easy to prepare, your guests will certainly be impressed.

PARSLEY

SERVES 4–6

175g/6oz dried wholewheat macaroni

dash of olive oil, plus extra for greasing

175g/6oz small cauliflower florets

275ml/½pt Tomato Sauce (page 9)

15g/½oz freshly grated Parmesan cheese

50g/2oz grated mature Cheddar cheese

2tbsp chopped fresh parsley

salt and freshly ground black pepper

5 large savoy cabbage leaves, stalks removed

fresh herbs, to garnish

Bring a large saucepan of water to the boil and add the macaroni with a dash of olive oil. Cook for about 10 minutes, stirring occasionally, until tender. Drain and set aside.

Meanwhile, blanch the cauliflower florets in boiling water, drain and place in a bowl.

Stir in the macaroni, Tomato Sauce, Parmesan and Cheddar cheeses, chopped parsley and season with salt and freshly ground black pepper. Allow to cool completely.

Preheat the oven to 180°C/350°F/Gas Mark 4. Blanch the cabbage leaves in boiling water, then drain and rinse under cold running water immediately. Pat dry with absorbent kitchen paper, then use to line a 1.1 litre/2pt greased pudding basin, overlapping the leaves and covering the base. Allow the leaves to hang over the sides of the basin.

Spoon the cool pasta mixture into the prepared basin, pressing down firmly with the back of the spoon. Fold the overhanging leaves over the top to encase the pasta filling. Cover the top of the basin with greased aluminium foil and bake in the centre of the oven for about 25–30 minutes. Leave to stand for 10 minutes before inverting on to a serving plate. Garnish with fresh herbs and serve.

Brassicas with Bavettini

This is a good store-cupboard recipe as any of the brassica family work well here. You could also vary the type of pasta used, according to what you have in your cupboard.

SERVES 4–6

450g/1lb dried bavettini (long, thin, flat shapes)

dash of olive oil, plus 45ml/3tbsp

3 cloves of garlic, crushed

1 onion, finely chopped

3tbsp chopped fresh rosemary

350g/12oz mixed brassicas, such as broccoli, cauliflower, kale and cabbage, chopped or shredded

salt and freshly ground black pepper

extra olive oil and freshly grated Parmesan cheese, to serve

Bring a large saucepan of water to the boil and add the bavettini with a dash of olive oil. Cook for about 10 minutes, stirring occasionally, until tender. Drain and set aside.

Heat the olive oil in a large frying pan and sauté the garlic, onion and rosemary for about 3 minutes, until the onion has softened.

Add the chopped or shredded brassicas and season with salt and freshly ground black pepper. Cook for about 10 minutes, until the vegetables are tender.

Toss in the cooked bavettini and cook for about 3 minutes, stirring frequently, until the brassicas have mixed in and the dish is heated through.

Serve drizzled with extra olive oil and sprinkled with freshly grated Parmesan.

Chinese Spring Greens with Fusilli

This quick-to-prepare, nutritious dish is perfect for a light lunch when entertaining friends.

SERVES 4–6

350g/12oz dried fusilli (small twists)

dash of olive oil

45ml/3tbsp sesame oil

3 cloves of garlic, crushed

100g/4oz carrots, peeled and cut into ribbons

150g/5oz spring greens, stalks removed and leaves shredded

75–90ml/5–6tbsp dark soya sauce

25g/1oz toasted sesame seeds

Bring a large saucepan of water to the boil and add the fusilli with a dash of olive oil. Cook for about 10 minutes, stirring occasionally, until the pasta is tender. Drain thoroughly and set aside.

Heat the sesame oil in a wok or large frying pan and add the garlic. Stir-fry for 30 seconds, then add the carrot ribbons. Continue to cook for 3–4 minutes, then add the shredded spring greens. Cook for 2–3 minutes, stirring continuously.

Stir in the soya sauce, sesame seeds and the fusilli. Cook for a further 2 minutes, and serve immediately.

FUSILLI

> **TIP:**
> To cut the carrots into wafer-thin ribbons, peel away the outside skin using a vegetable peeler, then continue peeling the carrot.

Stilton and Broccoli Soup with Tortelloni

A meal in itself, this recipe provides all the richness, flavour and hunger satisfaction your guests could possibly require.

SERVES 4–6

225g/8oz fresh tortelloni (choose your favourite filling)

dash of olive oil

50g/2oz butter

1 clove of garlic, crushed

450g/1lb broccoli spears, trimmed

1.1l/2pt vegetable stock

100g/4oz Stilton cheese, crumbled

salt and freshly ground black pepper

75ml/5tbsp single cream

Bring a large saucepan of water to the boil and add the tortelloni with a dash of olive oil. Cook for about 5 minutes, stirring occasionally, until tender. Drain and set aside.

Melt the butter in a large saucepan and sauté the garlic for about 2 minutes. Add the broccoli spears and continue to cook for about 5 minutes, stirring frequently.

Add the vegetable stock to the broccoli mixture and gradually bring the soup to the boil. Simmer for about 5 minutes, until the broccoli has softened. Purée the soup, in batches if necessary, in a food processor or blender until smooth.

Return the soup to the cleaned saucepan and place over gentle heat. Stir in the crumbled Stilton cheese and season with salt and freshly ground black pepper. Cook for about 3 minutes, until the cheese has melted. Stir in the cream and tortelloni. Cook for 2–3 minutes to heat through then serve immediately.

BROCCOLI

Pasta-stuffed Cabbage Leaves

Easy to prepare and sure to impress the guests, this dish can be made the day before and kept in the refrigerator. Allow an extra 15–20 minutes to reheat in the oven before serving.

TORTELLINI

SERVES 4

75g/3oz dried gnocchetti sardi (dumpling shapes) and/or pastina (any tiny shapes)

dash of olive oil

8 large savoy cabbage leaves, stalks removed

FOR THE FILLING:

30ml/2tbsp olive oil

2 cloves of garlic, crushed

2 carrots, peeled and grated

2 courgettes, grated

4 tomatoes, skinned, deseeded and chopped

50g/2oz chopped walnuts

salt and freshly ground black pepper

FOR THE SAUCE:

400g/14oz can chopped tomatoes

60ml/4tbsp dry red wine

150ml/¼pt vegetable stock

1tbsp dried oregano

1 onion, very finely chopped

salt and freshly ground black pepper

Bring a large saucepan of water to the boil and add the pasta with a dash of olive oil. Cook for about 10 minutes, stirring occasionally, until tender. Drain and set aside.

Blanch the cabbage leaves in boiling water, then quickly immerse in cold water and drain. Pat dry with absorbent kitchen paper and set aside.

To make the filling, heat the olive oil in a large frying pan and sauté the garlic for about 1 minute. Add the grated carrots and courgettes and cook for a further 3–4 minutes, stirring occasionally, until tender.

Add the chopped tomatoes, walnuts and pasta. Season with salt and freshly ground black pepper. Cook for about 5 minutes, stirring occasionally, then set aside to cool.

To make the sauce, place all the ingredients in a saucepan and bring to simmering point. Cook for 20–30 minutes, stirring occasionally, until reduced and thickened. Allow to cool slightly, then transfer to a food processor or blender and purée until smooth. Set aside. Preheat the oven to 200°C/400°F/Gas Mark 6.

To assemble the stuffed cabbage leaves, lay the blanched leaves out on the work surface, concave side uppermost, and divide the mixture between the leaves, placing it in the centre of each. Fold the edges of each leaf over to completely encase the filling, securing with a cocktail stick.

Arrange the stuffed leaves in a shallow ovenproof dish and pour the sauce around the edges. Cover with aluminium foil and bake for about 20 minutes, until heated through. Serve immediately, with any extra sauce served separately.

Lasagnette with Cauliflower and Broccoli

Ask for "mature Pecorino" or "Pecorino Sardo", which are hard cheeses. Alternatively, use Parmesan cheese.

SERVES 6

350g/12oz dried plain and tomato lasagnette (ruffle-edged ribbons)

dash of olive oil, plus 75ml/5tbsp

225g/8oz small cauliflower florets

225g/8oz small broccoli florets

2 cloves of garlic, crushed

75g/3oz freshly grated Pecorino cheese

pinch of freshly grated nutmeg

2tbsp chopped fresh parsley

salt and freshly ground black pepper

Bring a large saucepan of water to the boil and add the lasagnette with a dash of olive oil. Cook for about 10 minutes, stirring occasionally until tender. Drain and set aside, covered.

Bring two saucepans of water to the boil and add the cauliflower and broccoli florets. Cook for about 8–10 minutes, until tender. Drain and set aside.

Heat the olive oil in a frying pan and sauté the garlic for about 1 minute. Add the cauliflower, broccoli, lasagnette, about two-thirds of the Pecorino cheese, nutmeg and parsley and season with salt and freshly ground black pepper. Mix well, then transfer to a warm serving dish and sprinkle with the remaining Pecorino cheese. Serve immediately.

Spaghetti with Cauliflower Sauce

A cheesy change from the more traditional spaghetti sauces, this one will definitely have them coming back for more!

SERVES 4–6

450g/1lb dried spaghetti

dash of olive oil

25g/1oz butter

25g/1oz freshly grated Parmesan cheese

freshly ground black pepper

FOR THE SAUCE:

50g/2oz butter

2 cloves of garlic, crushed

3tbsp chopped fresh parsley

350g/12oz cauliflower florets, finely chopped

50g/2oz plain flour

275ml/½pt vegetable stock

275ml/½pt milk

salt and freshly ground black pepper

150g/5oz grated mature Cheddar cheese, plus extra, to serve

Bring a large saucepan of water to the boil and add the spaghetti with a dash of olive oil. Cook for about 10 minutes, stirring occasionally, until tender. Drain and return to the saucepan. Toss in the butter and Parmesan cheese. Season with freshly ground black pepper, then set aside, covered, to keep warm.

Melt the butter in a large saucepan and sauté the garlic and parsley for about 2 minutes, then add the cauliflower florets. Stir, cover and cook for about 8 minutes, until the cauliflower has softened slightly.

Stir in the flour, then gradually stir in the vegetable stock and the milk, stirring well after each addition to prevent any lumps.

Slowly bring the sauce to boiling point, stirring constantly, until thickened. Season with salt and freshly ground black pepper and stir in the grated Cheddar cheese. Cook for a further 2–3 minutes, stirring, until the cheese has melted. Serve the spaghetti on warmed individual plates with the cauliflower sauce, sprinkled with a little extra grated Cheddar cheese.

Cannelloni with Greens and Walnuts

Serve with a simple crisp, fresh salad to complement the rich, cheesy sauce and walnut filling. Fresh spinach is a good alternative for this recipe.

SERVES 4

12 dried cannelloni (tubes)

dash of olive oil

butter, for greasing

50g/2oz walnuts, chopped

FOR THE FILLING:

45ml/3tbsp olive oil

1 large onion, chopped

1 clove of garlic, crushed

450g/1lb spring greens, shredded

200g/7oz can chopped tomatoes

1tsp dried oregano

3tbsp chopped fresh basil

225g/8oz ricotta cheese

75g/3oz fresh wholemeal breadcrumbs

50g/2oz walnuts

good pinch of freshly grated nutmeg

salt and freshly ground black pepper

FOR THE CHEESE SAUCE:

25g/1oz butter

25g/1oz plain flour

275ml/½pt milk

50g/2oz grated Fontina cheese

Bring a large saucepan of water to the boil and add the cannelloni with a dash of olive oil. Cook for about 10 minutes, stirring occasionally, until tender. Drain and rinse under cold running water. Drain again, then pat dry with absorbent kitchen paper and set aside.

BASIL

To make the filling, heat the olive oil in a large frying pan and sauté the onion and garlic for 2–3 minutes, until the onion has softened. Add the spring greens, tomatoes and oregano. Continue to cook for about 5 minutes, stirring frequently, until the liquid has completely evaporated. Remove from the heat and leave to cool.

Place the spring greens mixture in a food processor or blender and add the basil, ricotta cheese, breadcrumbs, walnuts and nutmeg. Purée until smooth, then season with salt and freshly ground black pepper.

To make the sauce, melt the butter in a saucepan. Stir in the flour and cook for 1 minute. Gradually stir in the milk, and heat until bubbling and thickened. Stir in the grated Fontina cheese.

Preheat the oven to 190°C/375°F/Gas Mark 5. Butter the insides of a shallow oven-proof dish. Using a teaspoon, stuff each cannelloni with the filling then lay it in the dish.

Pour the cheese sauce evenly over the cannelloni. Sprinkle with walnuts and bake for about 30 minutes, until bubbling and golden.

TIP:

Sheets of fresh lasagne can be used instead of dried cannelloni. Make up ½ quantity Pasta Dough (page 8) and roll out to 5mm/¼inch thick. Cut into 10 × 15cm/4 × 6inch rectangles and spoon some of the filling along the short end of the sheet of pasta. Roll it up into a neat tube and place in the dish with the sealed end underneath.

Sprout Soup with Almonds

A warming soup with a subtle flavour, this makes an excellent starter for a dinner party. Made up to two days in advance, this soup can be reheated just before serving.

SERVES 4–6

50g/2oz butter

1 clove of garlic, crushed

2tsp chopped fresh rosemary

225g/8oz Brussels sprouts, finely shredded

100g/4oz dried ditalini rigati (tiny, short, ridged tubes)

50g/2oz toasted flaked almonds

1.4l/2½pt vegetable stock

salt and freshly ground black pepper

60ml/4tbsp single cream

freshly grated Parmesan cheese, to serve

Melt the butter in a large saucepan and sauté the garlic and rosemary for about 2 minutes. Add the shredded Brussels sprouts and cook for a further 3–4 minutes, stirring occasionally. Add the ditalini rigati with the flaked almonds. Stir and cook for 1–2 minutes, then stir in the vegetable stock and season with salt and freshly ground black pepper.

Cover the soup and simmer for about 10 minutes, stirring occasionally. Stir in the cream, then serve in individual bowls with freshly grated Parmesan cheese.

BRUSSELS SPROUTS

5 **Pasta** *with Various Vegetables*

Vegetable and Fresh Coriander Soup

A light, fresh-tasting soup that is ideal either as a starter or as a light lunch.

SERVES 4–6

1.1l/2pt vegetable stock

175g/6oz dried pasta (any shape)

dash of olive oil

100g/4oz carrots, thinly sliced

175g/6oz frozen peas

6tbsp chopped fresh coriander

salt and freshly ground black pepper

Bring the vegetable stock to the boil in a large saucepan and add the pasta with a dash of olive oil. Cook for about 5 minutes, stirring occasionally, then add the sliced carrots.

Cook for 5 minutes, then add the peas and coriander. Season with salt and freshly ground black pepper and simmer gently for about 10 minutes, stirring occasionally, until the pasta and carrots are tender. Serve the soup with finely grated cheese, if wished.

Minestrone Soup

There are many different versions of this classic soup; this one is simple, wholesome and filling. Serve with warm, crusty garlic bread.

CARROTS

SERVES 4–6

75ml/5tbsp extra virgin olive oil

3 cloves of garlic, crushed

450g/1lb carrots, peeled and finely diced

450g/1lb courgettes, finely diced

75g/3oz dried pastina (any tiny pasta shapes)

5tbsp chopped fresh parsley

50g/2oz vegetable purée

1.4l/2½pt good vegetable stock

salt and freshly ground black pepper

freshly grated Parmesan cheese, to serve

Heat the olive oil in a large saucepan and add the garlic. Sauté for about 2 minutes, then stir in the diced carrots and courgettes. Cook for about 5 minutes, stirring occasionally.

Stir the pastina and chopped parsley into the vegetable mixture, add the vegetable purée and vegetable stock and season with salt and freshly ground black pepper.

Cover and simmer for about 30 minutes, until the vegetables and pasta have softened and the flavours have developed. Serve with freshly grated Parmesan cheese.

Pasta Paella

Based on the classic recipe, this dish makes a delicious, nutritious alternative, using pasta as the main ingredient. Any pasta shape will do; even add a combination of shapes for extra texture.

FARFALLE

450g/1lb dried farfalle (bows)

1tsp ground turmeric

dash of olive oil, plus 45ml/3tbsp

2 cloves of garlic, crushed

1 Spanish onion

1 red pepper, seeded and chopped

100g/4oz baby carrots

100g/4oz baby sweetcorn

100g/4oz mangetout

100g/4oz fresh asparagus tips

75g/3oz black olives

15g/½oz plain flour

Bring a large saucepan of water to the boil and add the farfalle with the ground turmeric and a dash of olive oil. Cook for about 10 minutes, stirring occasionally, until tender. Drain, reserving the cooking liquid, and set aside.

Heat the remaining olive oil in a large frying pan and sauté the garlic and onion for about 3 minutes, until softened. Add the red pepper, carrots and sweetcorn and stir to combine. Cook for 2–3 minutes, then stir in the mangetout, asparagus tips, black olives and farfalle. Cook for 2–3 minutes, then sprinkle the flour over and mix into the vegetable mixture. Cook for 1 minute, then gradually stir in 425ml/¾pt of the reserved pasta cooking liquid. Cook for 2–3 minutes, until the sauce is bubbling and thickened. Serve straight from the pan or transfer to a warmed serving dish.

ASPARAGUS

Tagliarini with Green Beans and Garlic

A delicious summer salad,
hot main course or
vegetable accompaniment,
this dish is suitable for
almost any occasion.

ROTELLE

SERVES 4–6

350g/12oz dried tagliarini (flat spaghetti)

dash of olive oil, plus 60ml/4tbsp

350g/12oz haricot beans, topped and tailed

225g/8oz potato, cut into 1cm/½inch cubes

3 cloves of garlic, chopped

5tbsp chopped fresh sage

salt and freshly ground black pepper

freshly grated Parmesan cheese, to serve

Bring a large saucepan of water to the boil and add the tagliarini with a dash of olive oil. Cook for about 10 minutes, stirring occasionally, until tender. Drain and set aside.

Cook the beans and potato cubes in a large saucepan of boiling water for about 10 minutes, until tender. Drain well and set aside to keep warm.

Heat the remaining olive oil in a large frying pan, add the garlic and sage and season with salt and freshly ground black pepper. Sauté for 2–3 minutes, then add the cooked beans and potato. Cook for 1–2 minutes, then add the cooked tagliarini and mix well.

Cook for about 5 minutes, stirring occasionally, then transfer to a warmed serving dish. Sprinkle with freshly grated Parmesan cheese and serve.

Fettuccine with Garlicky Creamed Spinach

This tasty recipe is quick and easy to prepare. Serve immediately with plenty of freshly grated Parmesan cheese.

S E R V E S 4 – 6

450g/1lb dried fettuccine

dash of olive oil

25g/1oz butter

3 cloves of garlic, crushed

450g/1lb frozen chopped spinach, thawed and well drained

275ml/½pt single cream

pinch of freshly grated nutmeg

salt and freshly ground black pepper

50g/2oz freshly grated Parmesan cheese, plus extra to serve

Bring a large saucepan of water to the boil and add the fettuccine with a dash of olive oil. Cook for about 8 minutes, stirring occasionally, until tender. Drain and set aside, covered, to keep warm.

Melt the butter in a large frying pan and sauté the garlic for 1–2 minutes, then add the spinach. Cook over medium heat for about 5 minutes, stirring frequently, until the moisture has evaporated.

Add the cream and nutmeg and season with salt and freshly ground black pepper. Toss in the fettuccine and Parmesan cheese, stir and cook for a final minute. Serve with extra freshly grated Parmesan cheese.

Stuffed Courgettes

A delicious combination of tender courgette and fresh coriander mixed with a sweet soya sauce. You can make the filling and the sauce a day in advance. Reheat the sauce while the courgettes are baking.

SERVES 4–6

100g/4oz dried vermicelli (very thin spaghetti), broken into small pieces

dash of olive oil

4 medium-sized courgettes

finely chopped walnuts, to garnish

FOR THE FILLING:

150ml/¼pt sweet soya sauce

1 clove of garlic, crushed

50g/2oz mushrooms, very finely chopped

3tbsp fresh chopped coriander

25g/1oz shelled walnuts, very finely chopped

salt and freshly ground black pepper

FOR THE SAUCE:

60ml/4tbsp olive oil

2 cloves of garlic, crushed

25g/1oz chopped fresh coriander

salt and freshly ground black pepper

45ml/3tbsp vegetable stock

Bring a large saucepan of water to the boil and add the vermicelli with a dash of olive oil. Cook for about 5 minutes, stirring occasionally, until tender. Drain and set aside.

Cut a thin slice lengthways along the top of each courgette and chop this piece finely. Using a teaspoon, scoop out the flesh from the middle of the courgette and chop roughly. Arrange the hollowed courgettes in a shallow ovenproof dish and set aside. Preheat the oven to 200°C/400°F/Gas Mark 6.

To make the filling, place the sweet soya sauce and the garlic in a large frying pan and heat gently. Cook for about 1 minute, then stir in the mushrooms. Cook for about 5 minutes, stirring occasionally, then add the coriander. Cook for a further 2–3 minutes, then stir in the chopped walnuts and season to taste with salt and freshly ground black pepper. Simmer for 1–2 minutes, then stir in the cooked vermicelli.

Remove from the heat and, using a teaspoon, stuff the courgettes with the filling, placing any extra around the courgettes in the dish. Cover the dish with aluminium foil and bake for 25–30 minutes, until the courgettes are tender.

Meanwhile, to make the sauce, place all the ingredients in a food processor or blender and purée until smooth. Transfer to a small saucepan and heat gently until warm. Remove the stuffed courgettes from the oven and serve with the coriander sauce, garnished with finely chopped walnuts.

TARRAGON

Provençal Green Beans with Pasta

A delicious way to serve green beans, piping hot with freshly grated Parmesan cheese.

SERVES 4–6

30ml/2tbsp olive oil

3 cloves of garlic, crushed

1 onion, chopped

3tbsp chopped fresh thyme

450g/1lb haricot beans, topped and tailed

400g/14oz can chopped tomatoes

50g/2oz tomato purée

425ml/³⁄₄pt vegetable stock

150ml/¹⁄₄pt dry red wine

salt and freshly ground black pepper

450g/1lb dried pasta (any shapes)

25g/1oz butter

freshly grated Parmesan cheese

Heat the oil in a large frying pan and sauté the garlic and onion for about 3 minutes, until softened. Add the thyme, beans, tomatoes, tomato purée, vegetable stock and wine, season with salt and freshly ground black pepper and stir well to combine. Cover and cook gently for 25–30 minutes, until the beans are tender. Remove the cover and cook for a further 5–8 minutes, stirring occasionally, until the sauce has thickened slightly.

Meanwhile, bring a large saucepan of water to the boil and add the pasta with a dash of olive oil. Cook for about 10 minutes, stirring occasionally, until tender. Drain and return to the saucepan. Toss in butter and freshly ground black pepper.

Serve the beans with the hot, buttered pasta and freshly grated Parmesan cheese.

STELLETTI

Coconut Vegetables with Pasta

Make this dish a day ahead to allow the flavours to develop. Creamed coconut is available from most supermarkets and Indian grocers.

CARROTS

SERVES 4–6

45ml/3tbsp olive oil

2 cloves of garlic, crushed

1 onion, chopped

2tsp ground cumin

2tsp ground coriander

225g/8oz creamed coconut, chopped

700ml/1¼pt boiling water

salt and freshly ground black pepper

1 vegetable stock cube

225g/8 oz carrots, diced

225g/8oz courgettes, diced

5 sticks celery, chopped

½ small cauliflower, separated into florets

100g/4oz baby sweetcorn

5tbsp chopped fresh coriander

350g/12oz fresh linguini (thin, flat strips)

Heat the olive oil in a large frying pan and sauté the garlic, onion, cumin and coriander for about 3 minutes, stirring occasionally, until the onion has softened.

Add the creamed coconut to the boiling water. Stir well and season with salt and freshly ground black pepper. Add the stock cube and stir until dissolved.

Add the vegetables and coriander to the frying pan and stir well. Cover and simmer for 15–20 minutes, stirring occasionally, until the vegetables are tender. Remove the cover and continue to cook for about 5 minutes, until the sauce has thickened slightly.

Meanwhile, bring a large saucepan of water to the boil and add the linguini with a dash of olive oil. Cook for about 4 minutes, stirring occasionally, until tender. Drain and serve with the vegetables.

Pasta Baskets with Vegetables

The special piece of equipment used in this recipe is known by the French as a *nid d'oiseau* which, loosely translated, means a "bird's nest". It is a small metal basket in a basket on long handles, commonly used to make edible baskets of potato, filo pastry and, in this case, vermicelli.

100g/4oz dried vermicelli

dash of olive oil

vegetable oil, for deep-frying

FOR THE FILLING:

30ml/2tbsp sesame oil

2 cloves of garlic, crushed

100g/4oz baby sweetcorn

100g/4oz mangetout

2 carrots, thinly sliced

45ml/3tbsp soya sauce

1tbsp toasted sesame seeds

Bring a large saucepan of water to the boil and add the vermicelli with a dash of olive oil. Cook for about 5 minutes, stirring occasionally, until tender. Drain and set aside.

Heat the oil for deep frying and pack the cooked vermicelli into the bird's nest, if using. Otherwise fry the vermicelli in batches in a frying basket. Cook for 3–5 minutes in hot oil, until the vermicelli is crisp and golden. Remove the basket from the bird's nest and drain on absorbent kitchen paper. Repeat the process to make three more baskets. Arrange the baskets of loose vermicelli on individual serving plates. Set aside.

To make the filling, heat the sesame oil in a frying pan and sauté the garlic for 1–2 minutes. Add the sweetcorn, mangetout and carrots, stir and cook for 3–5 minutes, until tender. Stir in the soya sauce and sprinkle over the sesame seeds. Cook for a further 2 minutes, then spoon into the vermicelli baskets or on to a bed of vermicelli to serve.

CARROTS

Pea-green Ravioli with Cheese Sauce

Fresh mint tastes a million times better than dried, so do try to use it to give this dish the full flavour it deserves.

SERVES 6

⅔ quantity Pasta Dough (page 8), omitting the oil and water and adding 90ml/6tbsp spinach liquid instead

1 quantity Cheese Sauce (page 9)

FOR THE FILLING:

30ml/2tbsp olive oil

1 onion, very finely chopped

225g/8oz frozen peas

3tbsp chopped fresh mint

1 egg, beaten, for brushing with 2tsp tomato purée added

dash of olive oil

fresh mint sprigs, to garnish

Keep the fresh pasta dough covered with clingfilm at room temperature and the Cheese Sauce in a saucepan, ready to reheat.

To make the ravioli filling, heat the olive oil in a frying pan and sauté the onion for about 3 minutes, until softened. Add the frozen peas, cover and cook for about 7 minutes, stirring occasionally, until thawed and cooked through. Stir in the fresh mint and remove from the heat. Season with salt and freshly ground black pepper.

Allow the filling mixture to cool slightly, then transfer to a blender or food processor and purée until a slightly coarse texture is achieved. Cool the mixture completely.

To make the ravioli, cut the pasta dough in half. Roll out one half to a rectangle slightly larger than 35 × 25cm/14 × 10inches. Trim the edges of the dough neatly.

Cover the rectangle with clingfilm to prevent it drying out. Roll out the other half of the dough to the same measurements, but do not trim the edges. Cover with clingfilm.

Place half teaspoonfuls of the filling mixture in lines, spaced about 2cm/¾in apart, all over the trimmed rectangle of pasta dough. Brush the beaten egg lightly in lines around the filling mixture, to make the square shapes of the ravioli.

Lay the other rectangle of dough on top and, starting at one end, seal in the filling by lightly pressing the dough, pushing out any trapped air and gently flattening the filling to make little packets. Using a sharp knife or pastry wheel, cut down and across in lines around the filling to make the square ravioli.

To cook the ravioli, bring a large saucepan to the boil and add the ravioli with a dash of olive oil. Cook for about 5 minutes, stirring occasionally, until tender. Drain and set aside, covered, to keep warm.

Meanwhile, reheat the Cheese Sauce over gentle heat. Serve with the cooked ravioli and garnish with fresh mint.

> **TIP:**
> To make 90ml/6tbsp spinach liquid, cook 225g/8oz fresh chopped spinach leaves, washed and still damp, in a covered saucepan for 5 minutes, stirring frequently. Place the cooked spinach in a sieve and press out as much green liquid as possible. Add a little extra water to make up the quantity, if necessary.

RAVIOLI

Chinese Vegetables with Pasta Noodles

Any type of pasta noodles are suitable for this recipe. Prepare them and keep them warm for only a few minutes, during which time the vegetables are quickly prepared.

SERVES 3–4

30ml/2tbsp sesame oil

1tsp chopped fresh root ginger

2 cloves of garlic, crushed

50g/2oz chopped blanched almonds

6 spring onions, cut into 5cm/2inch lengths

225g/8oz mangetout

100g/4oz carrots, in 5cm/2inch lengths

1 red pepper, seeded and cut into thin strips

275ml/½pt vegetable stock

45ml/3tbsp rich soya sauce

45ml/3tbsp dry sherry

3tbsp arrowroot

100g/4oz beansprouts, washed and trimmed

salt and freshly ground black pepper

Heat the sesame oil in a wok or frying pan and stir-fry the ginger and garlic for 1 minute. Stir in the chopped almonds and all the vegetables. Stir-fry for 1–2 minutes, then add the vegetable stock, soya sauce and sherry. Mix well and continue to cook for a further 1–2 minutes.

Mix the arrowroot in a small bowl with 15ml/1tbsp cold water. When smooth and without lumps, stir into the vegetable mixture. Cook for 2 minutes, then add the beansprouts and season with salt and pepper. Cook for a final 1–2 minutes, until the sauce has thickened slightly. Serve with pasta noodles, cooked according to the manufacturer's instructions.

Creamy Leek and Pasta Flan

This dish is delicious both fresh out of the oven or served chilled on a hot summer's day with a crisp green salad.

SERVES 6-8

100g/4oz dried orecchiette (ears)

dash of olive oil, plus 45ml/3tbsp

a little flour, for dredging

350g/12oz puff pastry, thawed if frozen

2 cloves of garlic, crushed

450g/1lb leeks, washed, trimmed and cut into 2.5cm/1inch chunks

2tbsp chopped fresh thyme

2 eggs, beaten

150ml/¼pt single cream

salt and freshly ground black pepper

75g/3oz grated red Leicester cheese

Bring a large saucepan of water to the boil and add the orecchiette with a dash of olive oil. Cook for about 10 minutes, stirring occasionally, until tender. Drain and set aside.

Dredge the work surface with a little flour and roll out the pastry. Use to line a greased, 25cm/10inch loose-bottomed fluted flan ring. Place in the refrigerator to chill for at least 10 minutes.

Preheat the oven to 190°C/375°F/Gas Mark 5. Heat the remaining olive oil in a large frying pan and sauté the garlic, leeks and thyme for about 5 minutes, stirring occasionally, until tender. Stir in the orecchiette and continue to cook for a further 2–3 minutes.

Place the beaten eggs in a mixing jug and whisk in the cream and salt and freshly ground black pepper.

Transfer the leek and pasta mixture to the pastry case, spreading out evenly. Pour over the egg and cream mixture, then sprinkle over with cheese. Bake for 30 minutes, until the mixture is firm and the pastry is crisp.

Spinach and Mushroom Lasagne

Made in advance and put in the oven before the guests arrive, this is the perfect dish for entertaining. You can relax and enjoy the company while supper sees to itself.

SERVES 6

butter, for greasing

225g/8oz fresh lasagne

½ quantity Cheese Sauce (page 9)

50g/2oz freshly grated Parmesan cheese

FOR THE FILLING:

30ml/2tbsp olive oil

2 cloves of garlic, crushed

1 onion, chopped

225g/8oz mushrooms, sliced

675g/1½lb frozen spinach, thawed and well drained

good pinch of freshly grated nutmeg

450g/1lb full-fat soft cheese

salt and freshly ground black pepper

Make the filling first. Heat the olive oil in a large frying pan and sauté the garlic and onion for about 3 minutes. Add the mushrooms and continue to cook for about 5 minutes, stirring occasionally. Add the spinach and nutmeg and cook for about 5 minutes, then stir in the soft cheese and season with salt and freshly ground black pepper. Cook for 3–4 minutes, until the cheese has melted and blended with the spinach mixture. Preheat the oven to 200°C/400°F/Gas Mark 6.

To assemble the lasagne, butter a lasagne dish and place a layer of lasagne on the bottom. Spoon some of the spinach mixture evenly over it, then add another layer of lasagne. Continue layering the pasta and spinach mixture alternately until both are used up, then pour the Cheese Sauce evenly over the top.

Sprinkle the Parmesan cheese over the lasagne and bake for about 40 minutes, until golden and bubbling.

Asparagus Ravioli with Tomato Sauce

A dinner-party dish which can be made in advance – the ravioli can even be put in the freezer several weeks before the party and cooked from frozen. The sauce can be made several hours ahead and reheated before serving.

S E R V E S   6

⅔ quantity Pasta Dough with 15ml/1tbsp tomato purée beaten into the eggs (page 8)

1 quantity Tomato Sauce (page 9)

1 egg, beaten, for brushing

dash of olive oil

chopped fresh herbs, to garnish

FOR THE FILLING:

30ml/2tbsp olive oil

1 clove of garlic, crushed

1 onion, very finely chopped

225g/8oz fresh asparagus, very finely chopped

salt and freshly ground black pepper

Keep the fresh pasta dough covered with clingfilm at room temperature and the Tomato Sauce in a saucepan, ready to reheat before serving.

To make the filling, heat the olive oil in a frying pan and sauté the garlic and onion for about 3 minutes, until the onion has softened. Add the chopped fresh asparagus and season with salt and freshly ground black pepper. Sauté the asparagus mixture for about 10 minutes, until softened. Set aside and allow to cool completely.

To make the ravioli, cut the pasta dough in half. Roll out one half to a rectangle slightly larger than 35 × 25cm/14 × 10inches. Trim the edges of the dough neatly. Cover the rectangle with the clingfilm to prevent it drying out. Roll out the other half of the dough to the same measurements. Do not trim the edges.

Place half teaspoonfuls of the filling mixture in lines, spaced about 2cm/¾inch apart, all over the trimmed rectangle of pasta dough. Brush the beaten egg lightly, in lines around the filling mixture, to make the square shapes for the ravioli.

Lay the other rectangle of pasta dough on top and, starting at one end, seal in the filling by lightly pressing the dough, pushing out any trapped air and gently flattening the filling, making little packets. Using a sharp knife or pastry wheel, cut down and then across in lines around the filling to make the square ravioli shapes.

To cook the ravioli, bring a large saucepan of water to the boil and add the ravioli with a dash of olive oil. Cook for about 6 minutes, stirring occasionally, until tender. Drain and set aside.

Meanwhile, reheat the Tomato Sauce. Serve the ravioli with the Tomato Sauce, sprinkled with chopped fresh herbs.

ASPARAGUS

Verdi Vegetables with Vermicelli

A lovely summer recipe to be eaten warm or cold, with chunks of crusty French bread.

PARSLEY

SERVES 4–6

350g/12oz dried vermicelli (long, thin spaghetti)

dash of olive oil

25g/1oz butter

350g/12oz mangetout, sliced lengthways

225g/8oz courgettes, shredded lengthways

75g/3oz pimiento-stuffed olives, sliced

salt and freshly ground black pepper

2tbsp chopped fresh parsley

2tbsp chopped fresh mint

squeeze of fresh lime juice

TO GARNISH:

fresh herbs

lime slices

Bring a large saucepan of water to the boil and add the vermicelli with a dash of olive oil. Cook for about 5 minutes, stirring occasionally, until tender. Drain and set aside.

Melt the butter in a large frying pan and sauté the sliced mangetout and the courgettes for about 5 minutes, stirring occasionally.

Add the remaining ingredients except the lime juice to the vegetable mixture and cook for a further 5 minutes, stirring occasionally. Mix in the vermicelli and cook for 2–3 minutes, until heated through. Squeeze the fresh lime juice over the mixture and serve, garnished with fresh herbs and lime slices.

6 **Pasta** *with Pulses and Beans*

Lentil and Coriander Lasagne

You could make up two or three portions and freeze them uncooked. They cook beautifully from frozen at 190°C/375°F/Gas Mark 5 for 50–60 minutes.

SERVES 1

75g/3oz red lentils, washed and drained

1 onion, roughly chopped

425ml/¾pt boiling water

15ml/1tbsp olive oil, plus extra for greasing

1 clove of garlic, crushed

3tbsp chopped fresh coriander

75g/3oz mushrooms, sliced

10ml/2tsp sweet soya sauce

15ml/1tbsp tomato purée

salt and freshly ground black pepper

1 sheet fresh lasagne (approx 20 × 10cm/ 8 × 4inches), cut in half

½ quantity Cheese Sauce (page 9)

25g/1oz grated red Leicester cheese

Place the lentils and chopped onion in a large saucepan and add the boiling water. Bring to the boil, then simmer for about 15 minutes. Drain and set aside. Preheat the oven to 200°C/400°F/Gas Mark 6.

Heat the olive oil in a large frying pan and sauté the garlic and coriander for about 1 minute, then add the sliced mushrooms. Cook for about 4 minutes, then add the sweet soya sauce and tomato purée and season with salt and freshly ground black pepper. Add the cooked lentil mixture, stir and cook gently for about 5 minutes.

To assemble the lasagne, oil a shallow ovenproof dish and place one sheet of the lasagne on the bottom. Cover with half the lentil mixture, then add the other sheet of lasagne. Spoon the remaining lentil mixture over the top, spread out evenly, then pour the Cheese Sauce over the top. Sprinkle with grated cheese then bake for about 20 minutes.

> **TIP:**
>
> This is a perfect opportunity to use up any left-over home-made pasta from another recipe – it is not worth making up a fresh batch for this dish as it uses such a small amount.

ROTELLE

Corn and Butter Bean Bake

Canned beans are ideal for this recipe, so take advantage of their convenience.

FARFALLE

SERVES 4

75g/3oz dried farfallini (tiny bows)

dash of olive oil

45ml/3tbsp sunflower oil

2 cloves of garlic, crushed

1 onion, very finely chopped

3tbsp chopped fresh thyme

4 sticks celery, chopped

225g/8oz canned butter beans, drained

100g/4oz frozen sweetcorn kernels

1tbsp plain wholewheat flour

275ml/½pt vegetable stock

salt and freshly ground black pepper

FOR THE TOPPING:

2tbsp sesame seeds

2tbsp fresh wholewheat breadcrumbs

sesame oil, to drizzle

Bring a large saucepan of water to the boil and add the farfallini with a dash of olive oil. Cook for about 8 minutes, stirring occasionally, until tender. Drain and set aside. Preheat the oven to 180°C/350°F/Gas Mark 4.

Heat the sunflower oil in a large frying pan and sauté the garlic, onion and fresh thyme for about 3 minutes, until the onion has softened.

Add the chopped celery and cook for about 3 minutes, then add the butter beans and sweetcorn. Cook for about 5 minutes, stirring occasionally, then stir in the flour until evenly blended.

Gradually stir in the vegetable stock, stirring well then season with salt and freshly ground black pepper. Cook for about 5 minutes, then transfer the butter bean mixture to a shallow, ovenproof dish.

In a small bowl, combine the sesame seeds with the breadcrumbs, then sprinkle the mixture over the butter beans. Drizzle over a little sesame oil, then bake for about 20 minutes, until the topping is crisp. Serve immediately.

Spaghetti with Lentil Balls and Tomato Sauce

This is a great dish for the kids. Make double the amount of lentil balls and keep them, covered, in the refrigerator for several days for the kids to snack on. Serve with their favourite pasta for a fast, filling, nutritious dish.

SERVES 4–6

350g/12oz dried pasta (any shape)

dash of olive oil

sunflower oil, for deep-frying

400g/14oz can chopped tomatoes

FOR THE LENTIL BALLS:

100g/4oz green lentils, washed and drained

75g/3oz shelled walnuts or cashew nuts

1 bunch of spring onions, chopped

25g/1oz dried wholemeal breadcrumbs

15ml/1tbsp curry paste

salt and freshly ground black pepper

2 eggs, beaten

Bring a large saucepan of water to the boil and add the pasta with a dash of olive oil. Cook for about 10 minutes, stirring occasionally, until tender. Drain and return to the saucepan. Cover to keep warm.

To make the Lentil Balls, bring a large saucepan of water to the boil and add the lentils. Simmer for about 25 minutes, stirring occasionally, until softened. Drain well and allow to cool slightly.

Place the cooked lentils in a food processor or blender and add the nuts, spring onions, breadcrumbs, curry paste and salt and freshly ground black pepper. Purée until smooth, then gradually beat in the eggs to give a fairly firm mixture. Using slightly damp hands, roll the mixture into tiny balls and set aside on a baking sheet.

Heat the oil for deep-frying and cook the balls in batches for about 2 minutes, until crisp and cooked through. Drain on absorbent kitchen paper, then add to the pasta with a can of chopped tomatoes.

Place the saucepan over gentle heat to warm through, then serve immediately.

STELLETTI

Stuffed Pasta Shells

These are great as a starter or served as a canapé with drinks at a party. They can be made in advance and served cold or reheated in the oven to serve warm.

BASIL

SERVES 4–6

12 dried conchiglie rigate (large shells)

dash of olive oil

FOR THE FILLING:

225g/8oz brown lentils, washed and drained

2 cloves of garlic, crushed

400g/14oz can chopped tomatoes

15ml/1tbsp tomato purée

3tbsp chopped fresh basil

50ml/2floz dry red wine

salt and freshly ground black pepper

FOR THE TOPPING:

25g/1oz fine dried breadcrumbs

25g/1oz finely grated fresh Parmesan cheese

3tbsp chopped fresh parsley

Bring a large saucepan of water to the boil and add the conchiglie rigate with a dash of olive oil. Cook for about 10 minutes, stirring occasionally, until tender. Drain and rinse under cold running water. Drain again and lay out on absorbent kitchen paper.

To make the filling, bring a large saucepan of water to the boil and add the lentils. Simmer for about 30 minutes, until tender. Drain and rinse under boiling water.

Place the garlic, chopped tomatoes, tomato purée, fresh basil, wine and salt and freshly ground black pepper in a large frying pan. Bring to boiling point, then reduce the heat and simmer for 2–3 minutes. Add the lentils, stir and cook for about 10 minutes, until the moisture has evaporated and the mixture has thickened.

Use a teaspoon to stuff the pasta shells with the filling mixture and arrange them on a baking sheet. Combine the topping ingredients in a small bowl and sprinkle over the stuffed shells. Place under a hot grill for about 5 minutes, until golden.

Eastern Pasta Salad

A traditional combination of mint and lemon makes this dish a salad for summer. Choose your favourite pasta shapes for this recipe and serve with warm pitta bread to mop up the delicious dressing.

SERVES 4–6

350g/12oz dried pasta

dash of olive oil

400g/14oz can chickpeas, drained

4tbsp chopped fresh mint

finely grated zest of 1 lemon

FOR THE DRESSING:

3 cloves of garlic, crushed

90ml/6tbsp extra virgin olive oil

45ml/3tbsp white wine vinegar

freshly squeezed juice of 1 lemon

salt and freshly ground black pepper

Bring a large saucepan of water to the boil and add the pasta with a dash of olive oil. Cook for about 10 minutes, stirring occasionally, until tender. Drain and rinse under cold running water. Drain again and place in a large mixing bowl.

Add the chickpeas, mint and lemon zest to the pasta. Place all the dressing ingredients in a screw-top jar and shake well to mix. Pour the dressing over the chickpea mixture and mix well to combine. Cover and chill for at least 30 minutes. Toss before serving.

CHICK PEAS

Pasta Bean Soup

A nutritious meal in itself – low-fat and full of protein. Serve with warm, crusty garlic bread.

PARSLEY

SERVES 4–6

30ml/2tbsp olive oil

3 cloves of garlic, crushed

4tbsp chopped fresh parsley

150g/5oz dried wholewheat gnocchi piccoli (shells)

1.4l/2½pt vegetable stock

45ml/3tbsp vegetable or tomato purée

400g/14oz can mixed beans, such as borlotti, kidney, cannellini etc, drained

salt and freshly ground black pepper

freshly grated Parmesan cheese, to serve

Heat the olive oil in a large saucepan and sauté the garlic with the chopped parsley for about 2 minutes. Add the gnocchi piccoli and cook for 1–2 minutes, stirring constantly.

Pour in the vegetable stock and add the vegetable or tomato purée. Bring to the boil, reduce the heat then simmer for about 10 minutes, stirring occasionally, until the pasta is tender.

Add the beans and season with salt and freshly ground black pepper. Continue to cook for a further 5 minutes, then serve with a little freshly grated Parmesan cheese.

OPPOSITE *Pasta Bean Soup.*

Fusilli with Kidney Beans

The chilli flavouring in this dish can be adjusted according to taste.

SERVES 4–6

450g/1lb dried fusilli (short twists)

dash of olive oil

2 × 400g/14oz cans chopped tomatoes

1 onion, sliced

3tbsp chopped fresh parsley

pinch of chilli powder

salt and freshly ground black pepper

30ml/2tbsp tomato purée

150ml/¼pt dry red wine

400g/14oz can red kidney beans

Bring a large saucepan of water to the boil and add the fusilli with a dash of olive oil. Cook for about 10 minutes, stirring occasionally, until tender. Drain and set aside.

Place all the remaining ingredients except the kidney beans in a large frying pan and bring to boiling point. Reduce the heat and simmer for about 10 minutes, until the liquid has reduced and the onion has softened.

Add the fusilli and kidney beans to the tomato mixture. Stir, cover and cook for about 5 minutes, stirring occasionally. Serve immediately.

KIDNEY BEANS

Lentil Pasta Burgers

Served with pitta bread and a little salad, these make a treat for children.

TORTELLINI

SERVES 2-4

75g/3oz dried pastina (any tiny shapes)

dash of olive oil

200g/7oz can brown lentils, drained

25g/1oz dried wholemeal breadcrumbs

25g/1oz finely grated fresh Parmesan cheese

1 small onion, chopped

1tbsp chopped fresh parsley

60ml/4tbsp crunchy peanut butter

15ml/1tbsp tomato purée

1tsp yeast extract

60ml/4tbsp hot water

sunflower oil, for shallow frying

Bring a large saucepan of water to the boil and add the pastina with a dash of olive oil. Cook for about 8 minutes, stirring occasionally, until tender. Drain and allow to cool slightly.

Combine the pasta in a large mixing bowl with the lentils, breadcrumbs, Parmesan cheese, onion and parsley.

Place the peanut butter, tomato purée and yeast extract in a separate bowl and stir together with the hot water. Add this to the lentil mixture and mix well.

Using damp hands, divide the mixture into four equal portions and form into burger shapes. Heat the oil for shallow frying and fry the burgers for about 5 minutes on each side. Serve hot or cold.

> **TIP:**
> The Lentil Pasta Burgers can also be grilled, if you prefer. Place on a lightly oiled baking sheet and put under a preheated grill for about 3–5 minutes on each side.

Lentil and Mushroom Cannelloni

The tomato cannelloni is not essential, but adds to the attractive colour of the finished dish. Dried cannelloni tubes work just as well.

SERVES 4

⅓ quantity Pasta Dough (page 8), with 15ml/1tbsp tomato purée beaten into the eggs

dash of olive oil, plus 45ml/3tbsp

225g/8oz brown lentils, washed and drained

3 cloves of garlic, crushed

2tbsp dried thyme

2 × quantity Mushroom Sauce (page 9)

75g/3oz grated Cheddar cheese

chopped fresh parsley, to garnish

Roll out the pasta dough thinly to a 40cm/16inch square and cut it into four 10cm/4inch wide strips. Cut the strips across to make 16 squares.

Bring a large saucepan of water to the boil and add the squares of pasta, in batches, with a dash of olive oil. Cook for about 3 minutes, until tender. Drain and rinse under cold running water. Pat dry with absorbent kitchen paper and set aside.

Bring another large saucepan of water to the boil and add the lentils. Cook for about 30 minutes, stirring occasionally, until tender. Drain and rinse under boiling water. Drain again and set aside. Preheat the oven to 180°C/350°F/Gas Mark 4.

Heat the remaining olive oil in a large frying pan and sauté the garlic and thyme for about 2 minutes. Add the lentils, stir and cook for about 5 minutes. Remove from the heat and set aside to cool slightly.

Place a little of the lentil mixture along one edge of each piece of pasta and roll up to form a neat tube. Arrange the cannelloni in a shallow ovenproof dish, seal sides down. Pour the Mushroom Sauce over the cannelloni and sprinkle with grated cheese. Bake for about 40 minutes, until bubbling and golden. Serve garnished with chopped fresh parsley.

Bean Curry with Lasagnette

Lasagnette is a longer, thinner version of lasagne. Any form of noodles work well to serve with this recipe.

275g/10oz lasagnette (long, thin strips with crinkled edges)

dash of olive oil, plus 2tbsp

2 cloves of garlic, crushed

1 onion, chopped

45–60ml/3–4tbsp mild curry paste

3tbsp chopped fresh coriander

275ml/½pt vegetable stock

2 × 400g/14oz cans mixed beans, such as black-eyed, flageolet, cannellini etc, drained

chopped fresh coriander

lime slices, to garnish

Bring a large saucepan of water to the boil and add the lasagnette with a dash of olive oil. Cook for about 10 minutes, stirring occasionally, until tender. Drain and return to the saucepan. Cover, to keep warm.

Heat the remaining olive oil in a large saucepan and sauté the garlic and onion for about 5 minutes, stirring occasionally. Stir in the curry paste and cook for a further 2–3 minutes. Add the chopped coriander and vegetable stock and cook for 5 minutes. Stir in the beans, cover and cook for 10 minutes, stirring occasionally.

Serve the curry with the lasagnette, sprinkled with chopped fresh coriander and garnished with lime slices.

FLAGEOLET BEANS

Sautéed Flageolet Beans with Fusilli

A garlicky dish, made with fresh tarragon to enhance the delicate flavours. Serve as a main course or as an accompaniment.

SERVES 2–4

275g/10oz dried fusilli (short twists)

dash of olive oil, plus 60ml/4tbsp

3 cloves of garlic, crushed

1 large onion, sliced

2tbsp chopped fresh tarragon

400g/14oz can flageolet beans, drained

salt and freshly ground black pepper

Bring a large saucepan of water to the boil and add the fusilli with a dash of olive oil. Cook for about 10 minutes, stirring occasionally, until tender. Drain and set aside.

Heat the olive oil in a large frying pan and sauté the garlic and onion for about 5 minutes, until the onion has browned slightly. Add the tarragon and beans and season with salt and freshly ground black pepper. Cook for 2–3 minutes, then stir in the fusilli. Cook for 3–5 minutes, to heat through. Serve with a crisp green salad.

Winter Stew

You can give this vegetarian dish to carnivores – they'll never notice the lack of meat.

SERVES 4

100g/4oz dried wholewheat radiatori (radiators)

dash of olive oil, plus 30ml/2tbsp

2 cloves of garlic, crushed

1 onion, chopped

450g/1lb carrots, cut into 1cm/½in chunks

225g/8oz button mushrooms

400g/14oz can chopped tomatoes

2 × 400g/14oz cans red and black kidney beans, drained

275ml/½pt vegetable stock

1tbsp paprika

30ml/2tbsp sweet soya sauce

salt and freshly ground black pepper

1tbsp cornflour

KIDNEY BEANS

Bring a large saucepan of water to the boil and add the radiatori with a dash of olive oil. Cook for about 10 minutes, stirring occasionally, until tender. Drain and set aside.

Heat the remaining olive oil in a large saucepan and sauté the garlic and onion for about 3 minutes, stirring occasionally. Add the carrots and cook for about 5 minutes.

Add the mushrooms and continue to cook for about 3 minutes, stirring occasionally, until slightly softened. Add the remaining ingredients except the cornflour and stir in the radiatori. Cover and cook gently for about 15 minutes, until the vegetables are tender.

In a small bowl, mix the cornflour with a little of the cooking liquid to make a smooth paste. Add the cornflour paste to the stew. Stir and allow to boil again, stirring constantly, until thickened. Cook for a final 3 minutes before serving.

Sautéed Flageolet Beans with Fusilli.

Tagliatelle with Lentil Sauce

Here's a good store-cupboard recipe you can rustle up in minutes.

SERVES 4

350g/12oz dried tagliatelle

dash of olive oil

25g/1oz butter

FOR THE SAUCE:

30ml/2tbsp olive oil

2 cloves of garlic, crushed

1 large onion, very finely chopped

225g/8oz red lentils, washed and drained

45ml/3tbsp tomato purée

salt and freshly ground black pepper

575ml/1pt boiling water

sprigs of fresh rosemary, to garnish

freshly grated Parmesan cheese, to serve

Bring a large saucepan of water to the boil and add the tagliatelle with a dash of olive oil. Cook for about 10 minutes, stirring occasionally, until tender. Drain and return to the saucepan. Add the butter and stir. Cover and set aside, to keep warm.

To make the lentil sauce, heat the olive oil in a large saucepan and sauté the garlic and onion for about 5 minutes, stirring occasionally, until softened. Add the lentils, tomato purée, salt and freshly ground black pepper and stir in the boiling water. Bring to the boil, then simmer for about 20 minutes, stirring occasionally, until the lentils have softened.

Reheat the tagliatelle gently for 2–3 minutes, if necessary, then serve with the lentil sauce. Scatter over a few sprigs of fresh rosemary and serve with freshly grated Parmesan cheese.

Store-cupboard Salad

Use tiny pasta shapes for this salad and serve with warm, crusty French bread.

FLAGEOLET BEANS

SERVES 4–6

100g/4oz dried pastina (tiny shapes)

dash of olive oil

400g/14oz can mixed beans, such as kidney, cannellini, flageolet etc, drained

1 red pepper, seeded and very finely diced

2tsp dried oregano

FOR THE DRESSING:

2 cloves of garlic, crushed

60ml/4tbsp extra virgin olive oil

30–45ml/2–3tbsp balsamic vinegar

5ml/1tsp tomato purée

salt and freshly ground black pepper

Bring a large saucepan of water to the boil and add the pastina with a dash of olive oil. Cook for about 8 minutes, stirring occasionally, until tender. Drain and rinse under cold running water. Drain again and place in a large mixing bowl.

Add the beans, red pepper and oregano to the pasta. Place all the dressing ingredients in a screw-top jar and shake well to combine. Pour the dressing over the salad, toss and chill for at least 30 minutes before serving.

Continental Lentil Soup

Canned lentils make this soup even easier to prepare. They are available from most good delicatessens.

FUSILLI

SERVES 4–6

50g/2oz butter

2 cloves of garlic, crushed

75g/3oz dried pastina (any tiny shapes)

4tbsp finely chopped fresh parsley

400g/14oz can brown lentils, drained

1.4l/2½pt vegetable stock

salt and freshly ground black pepper

freshly grated Parmesan cheese, to serve (optional)

Melt the butter in a large saucepan and sauté the garlic for about 2 minutes, stirring occasionally.

Add the pastina and chopped parsley and stir. Cook for a further 2–3 minutes, then add the lentils and stock and season with salt and freshly ground black pepper.

Bring the soup to the boil, then reduce the heat and simmer for about 15 minutes. Serve with a little freshly grated Parmesan cheese, if wished.

7   **Pasta** *Puddings*

Baked Pasta Pudding

A nursery pudding which will probably become a firm favourite with the adults.

FIGS

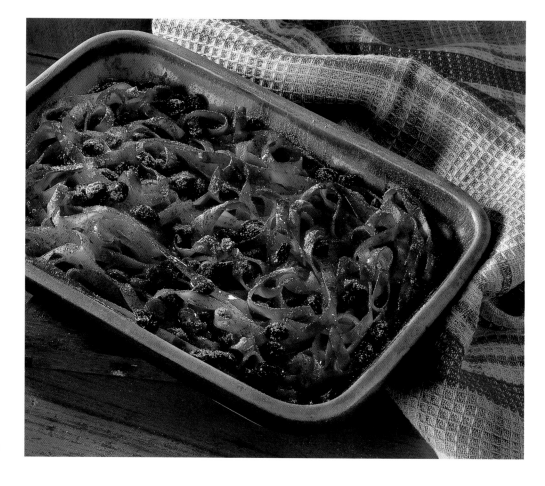

SERVES 4

100g/4oz dried tagliatelle

dash of sunflower oil

50g/2oz butter

2 eggs

100g/4oz caster sugar

pinch of ground cinnamon

grated zest of 1 lemon

few drops of vanilla essence

4tbsp sultanas

sifted icing sugar, to decorate

Preheat the oven to 190°C/375°F/Gas Mark 5. Bring a large saucepan of water to the boil and add the tagliatelle with a dash of sunflower oil. Cook for about 10 minutes, stirring occasionally, until tender. Drain and rinse under cold running water. Drain again and set aside.

Place the butter in a shallow ovenproof dish and melt in the oven for about 5 minutes. Remove from the oven and carefully swirl the melted butter around the sides of the dish. Set aside to cool slightly.

In a mixing bowl, whisk together the eggs and sugar until thick and frothy. Whisk in the cinnamon, lemon zest, vanilla essence and reserved melted butter. Stir in the sultanas and cooked tagliatelle until evenly coated in the egg mixture.

Transfer the pudding mixture to the prepared dish and distribute evenly. Bake for about 35–40 minutes, until the mixture has set and is crisp and golden. Allow to cool slightly. Serve warm, decorated with sifted icing sugar.

Honey, Orange and Almond Tagliatelle

Here's a really quick and easy dessert. Pasta tossed in butter and honey syrup makes a perfect pasta pudding.

SERVES 4–6

225g/8oz dried egg tagliatelle

dash of sunflower oil

4 oranges

75ml/5tbsp clear honey

25g/1oz soft light brown sugar

15ml/1tbsp lemon juice

40g/1½oz butter

75g/3oz flaked almonds

Bring a large saucepan of water to the boil and add the tagliatelle with a dash of sunflower oil. Cook for about 8–10 minutes, stirring occasionally, until tender. Drain and set aside.

While the pasta is cooking, peel and slice three of the oranges and cut the slices in half. Squeeze the juice from the remaining orange into a small saucepan. Add the honey, sugar and lemon juice. Bring to the boil, stirring to dissolve the sugar, and simmer for 1–2 minutes, until syrupy.

Melt the butter in a large frying pan and fry the flaked almonds until golden. Stir in the tagliatelle and honey syrup, heat through, then quickly stir in the orange slices. Serve immediately.

> **TIP:**
> Pare strips of zest from the skin of one orange and cut into thin "julienne" strips for decoration.

Chocolate Pasta Torte

A decadently rich dessert to serve on special occasions. Use good-quality plain dessert chocolate – ordinary cooking chocolate just won't taste the same.

SERVES 8

150g/5oz dried vermicelli (thin spaghetti)

dash of sunflower oil, plus extra for greasing

350g/12oz plain chocolate, broken into pieces

60ml/4tbsp water

100g/4oz unsalted butter

100g/4oz caster sugar

finely grated zest of 1 orange

225g/8oz can unsweetened chestnut purée

60ml/4tbsp brandy

50g/2oz ground almonds

50g/2oz flaked almonds

75ml/5tbsp double cream

chocolate leaves, to decorate

Bring a large saucepan of water to the boil and add the vermicelli with a dash of sunflower oil. Cook for about 6 minutes, stirring occasionally, until tender. Drain and rinse under cold running water. Drain again and set aside.

Lightly oil a 18cm/7inch round springform or loose-bottomed cake tin and line with greaseproof paper. Lightly oil the paper.

Place 225g/8oz chocolate and the water in a small saucepan and heat gently until melted. Set aside to cool.

Meanwhile, cream together the butter, caster sugar and orange zest until light and fluffy, then gradually beat in the chestnut purée.

Add the melted chocolate to the brandy and mix well. Stir in the almonds and cooked vermicelli. Turn the mixture into the prepared tin and smooth over the surface. Refrigerate overnight.

Put the remaining chocolate and the cream into a small bowl over a saucepan of simmering water and heat gently, stirring occasionally, until melted and smooth. Remove the bowl from the heat.

Remove the torte from the tin and place on a wire cooling rack. Pour the melted chocolate mixture evenly over the cake, using a palette knife to coat the sides. Leave to set.

Carefully transfer the torte to a serving plate and decorate with chocolate leaves.

> **TIP:**
> To make chocolate leaves, melt 50g/2oz white or milk dessert chocolate in a small bowl over a saucepan of simmering water. Using a small brush, paint the melted chocolate on to the backs of a selection of small leaves. Arrange on a baking sheet lined with greaseproof paper and leave to set for at least 2 hours at room temperature. Carefully peel away the leaves and discard.

PEARS

Fruit Ravioli with a Red Coulis

Look out for dried mango and pineapple in health food shops and delicatessens. Alternatively use a mixture of chopped glacé fruits in this recipe.

SERVES 6–8

FOR THE FILLING:

100g/4oz no-soak dried apricots, finely chopped

100g/4oz dried mango or pineapple, finely chopped

finely grated zest of 1 orange

½tsp ground cinnamon

30ml/2tbsp amaretto liqueur (optional)

⅔ quantity Pasta Dough (page 8), (omitting the salt, using 15ml/1tbsp fresh orange juice instead of the water and adding the finely grated zest of 1 orange to the eggs)

lightly beaten egg

dash of sunflower oil

FOR THE COULIS:

350g/12oz fresh raspberries

50g/2oz icing sugar, sifted

TO DECORATE:

finely chopped pistachio nuts

fresh raspberries

mint sprigs

First make the filling; mix together the apricots, dried mango or pineapple, orange zest and cinnamon and set aside. Add the amaretto if desired.

To make the ravioli, cut the pasta dough in half and roll out one half to a 35 × 25cm/ 14 × 10inch rectangle. Trim the edges of the dough and cover with clingfilm to prevent it from drying out.

Roll out the other piece of pasta dough to the same size. Place half teaspoonfuls of the filling mixture in lines 2cm/¾inch apart on one piece of dough. Lightly brush beaten egg between the filling mixture and carefully lay the second piece of dough over the top. Starting at one end, press the dough down around the filling, carefully pushing out any trapped air. Using a sharp knife, pastry wheel or round cutter, cut in lines between the filling to divide the ravioli into squares.

Cook the ravioli in a large saucepan of boiling water with a dash of sunflower oil for about 5 minutes, stirring occasionally, until tender. Drain and set aside to cool slightly.

Meanwhile, make the coulis; place the raspberries and icing sugar in a food processor or blender and purée until smooth. Sieve to remove the seeds.

Serve the ravioli on individual plates with the coulis and decorate with chopped pistachio nuts, fresh raspberries and mint sprigs.

RASPBERRIES

Chocolate Pasta with Chocolate Sauce

A chocoholic's dream – it has to be tasted to be believed!

SERVES 6

⅔ quantity Pasta Dough (page 8), (omitting the salt and adding 25g/1oz cocoa powder and 25g/1oz icing sugar to the flour)

dash of sunflower oil

FOR THE SAUCE:

175g/6oz plain chocolate, broken into pieces

150ml/¼pt milk

30ml/2tbsp golden syrup

25g/1oz butter

TO DECORATE:

fresh strawberries

amaretti biscuits

FIGS

Keep the pasta dough wrapped in clingfilm to prevent it from drying out and set aside.

To make the sauce, place all the ingredients in a small saucepan and heat gently, stirring, for about 5 minutes, until melted, smooth and shiny. Cool slightly.

Roll out the pasta dough thinly on a floured surface and cut into rounds with a 5cm/2inch round plain or fluted cutter. Pinch the sides of each dough round together, pleating in the middle to make a bow shape. Set the bows aside on baking sheets lined with greaseproof paper.

To cook the pasta bows, bring a large saucepan of water to the boil and add the pasta with a dash of sunflower oil. Cook for about 3 minutes, stirring occasionally, until tender. Drain and return to the saucepan.

Pour the chocolate sauce over the pasta and stir gently to coat.

Winter Fruit Compote with Tiny Pasta Shapes

Try this for breakfast. It needs to be started the day before and will keep for several days in the refrigerator. Make up your own selection of mixed dried fruit, if you prefer.

SERVES 4–6

100g/4oz dried apricots

100g/4oz dried apple rings

100g/4oz dried pears

100g/4oz dried figs

50g/2oz dried cherries

4 cloves

2 allspice berries

1 stick of cinnamon

finely grated zest and juice of 1 orange

275ml/½pt weak tea

150ml/¼pt water

15g/½oz soft brown sugar

40g/1½oz dried pastina (any tiny shapes)

Place the dried fruit in a bowl with the spices, orange zest and juice, tea and water. Cover and leave to soak overnight.

The next day, spoon the compote into a saucepan, bring to the boil and simmer for 15 minutes, adding a little more water if necessary. Stir in the brown sugar and pastina and cook for a further 8–10 minutes, until the pastina is tender. Serve warm or cold.

PEARS

Cinnamon Fettuccine
with Apple and Cinnamon Sauce

A lovely autumn pudding, delicious served with cream. Ground mixed spice makes a good alternative to cinnamon.

SERVES 6

⅔ quantity Pasta Dough (page 8), (omitting the salt and adding 2tsp ground cinnamon to the flour)

FOR THE SAUCE:

450g/1lb dessert apples, peeled, cored and sliced

finely grated zest of 1 lemon

¼tsp ground cinnamon

45ml/3tbsp water, plus 150ml/¼pt

25g/1oz soft light brown sugar

75g/3oz sultanas

15g/½oz butter, plus a little extra

2tsp arrowroot blended with 10ml/2tsp cold water

flour, to dredge

dash of sunflower oil

Keep the pasta dough wrapped in clingfilm to prevent it from drying out and set aside.

To make the sauce, put the apples into a saucepan with the lemon zest, cinnamon and 45ml/3tbsp water. Cover and cook gently until the apples have softened. Remove about half of the apple slices from the saucepan and set aside. Place the remaining apples in a food processor or blender and purée until smooth.

Return the purée to the saucepan and stir in the reserved apples, sugar, sultanas, 15g/½oz butter, arrowroot mixture and 150ml/¼pt water. Cook for about 5 minutes, stirring constantly, until bubbling and thickened. Set aside.

To make the fettuccine, roll out the pasta dough very thinly on a floured surface. Lightly dredge with flour, then roll up and use a sharp knife to cut the dough into ½cm/¼ inch wide slices. Shake out the noodles as they are cut and pile them on a floured baking tray.

To cook the fettuccine, bring a large saucepan of water to the boil and add the pasta with a dash of sunflower oil. Cook for about 3 minutes, stirring occasionally, until tender.

Meanwhile, reheat the sauce. Drain the fettuccine and toss with a little extra butter. Stir in the sauce and serve on warmed individual plates.

TIP:
For a special occasion sprinkle each plate of pasta with a little calvados or rum before serving.

RASPBERRIES

Index

TARRAGON